"BRING THE CLASSICS TO LIFE"

Ivanhoe

LEVEL 5

Series Designer
Philip J. Solimene

Editor
Laura Machynski

Long Island, New York

Story Adaptors
Ed and Paula Teeling

Author
Sir Walter Scott

PREFACE

This story opens in merry England in the year 1194 toward the end of the reign of King Richard I, also known as Richard the Lion-Hearted.

In 1192, King Richard, returning home during the crusade, was captured by the cruel Duke of Austria and sent to prison, where he was held for ransom.

During Richard's absence, Prince John, Richard's brother, rules the land.

Copyright © 1993
A/V Concepts Corp.
Long Island, New York

Printed in U.S.A.
ISBN# 1-55576-099-6

CONTENTS

Words Used 4, 5

WORDS USED

Story 51	Story 52	Story 53	Story 54	Story 55
KEY WORDS				
armor	defeat	advise	mercy	attend
blond	helmet	nimble	severe	delay
bog	mighty	otherwise	slash	heal
cloak	shield	purse	sunk	release
merchant	thrust	repay	thrown	separate
tournament	yelp	squire	vicious	splendid
NECESSARY WORDS				
abbey	jousting		herald	art
jester	noble			dungeon
lance				outlaw
prior				yeoman

WORDS USED

Story 56	Story 57	Story 58	Story 59	Story 60
		KEY WORDS		
balcony	cell	concern	accompany	cape
broad	consider	failure	elm	drain
clerk	plead	glory	occasion	lurch
consent	presence	justice	pierce	monk
traitor	sob	oppose	seek	pardon
twilight	trial	volunteer	solid	torch
		NECESSARY WORDS		
friar	combat	crossroad	clanking	baron
	guilty		confession	coffin
	kidnapped		description	heir
				inheritance

Saxon Meets Norman

PREPARATION

Key Words

armor   (är´mər)   a covering worn to protect the body against weapons
The arrow could not damage his suit of <u>armor</u>.

blond   (blond)   a golden color; pale yellow
Lucy has long, <u>blond</u> pigtails.

bog   (bog)   soft, watery ground
The children wore their boots to walk through the <u>bog</u>.

cloak   (klōk)   a loose outer garment, usually sleeveless
Jane wore her <u>cloak</u> to school yesterday.

merchant   (mür´chənt)   a person who buys and sells goods for profit
It was time for the <u>merchant</u> to count up his money.

tournament   (tėr´nə mənt)   a sport long ago in which mounted and armored men fought against each other with lances or swords; contest of many persons in some sport
Many brave men fought in the <u>tournament</u>.

Saxon Meets Norman

Necessary Words

abbey	(ab´ ē)	the building or buildings where monks (churchmen) or nuns live

> *We went to the <u>abbey</u> to visit our good friend, Cyril.*

jester	(jes´ tər)	a fool in the courts of the Middle Ages

> *The <u>jester</u> performed tricks for the crowd.*

lance	(lans)	a weapon with a long wooden shaft and a sharp metal head

> *The knight used his <u>lance</u> to strike his enemy.*

prior	(pri´ ər)	the superior officer in the monastery

> *Monks obey their <u>prior</u>.*

Events

Crusade was a holy war.

People

Prior Aymer is a churchman.

Cedric of Rotherwood is a Saxon lord.

King Richard is a Norman king.

Knight Templar is a member of a religious and military order called the Knights Templar.

Prince John is the brother of King Richard.

William is the Norman prince who conquered England in 1066.

Saxon was an earlier conquering tribe of Britain.

Norman was a later conquering tribe of Britain.

Places

Austria is a country in central Europe.

Rotherwood is the landed estate of the Saxon lord.

Sherwood Forest is the well known forest-home of the famous outlaw Robin Hood.

Saxon Meets Norman

Eager to find shelter from the coming storm, Gurth and Wamba round up the pigs.

Preview:
1. Read the name of the story.
2. Look at the picture.
3. Read the sentence under the picture.
4. Read the first four paragraphs of the story.
5. Then answer the following question.

You learned from your preview that Gurth and Wamba were
___ a. Saxon lords.
___ b. rich kings.
___ c. knights in armor.
___ d. servants of Cedric of Rotherwood.

Turn to the Comprehension Check on page 10 for the right answer.

Now read the story.

Read to find out who the pilgrim turns out to be.

Saxon Meets Norman

Dark clouds cracked with lightning and began to cover the pink western sky. Thunder rolled down through the green hills of Sherwood Forest. A strange pair of companions drove a herd of pigs before them. They were eager to escape the coming storm. Both were servants of Cedric of Rotherwood, the Saxon lord whose lands bordered the forest.

Gurth, the herdsman, wore a tunic, or jacket, of rough goat skin from neck to knee. He carried a long knife and hunting horn in his belt. His face was fierce and he growled when he spoke.

His companion was small of build and light hearted. He was Wamba, the jester. He wore a cloth tunic of bright purple and a short red cloak with yellow lining. He wore silver bracelets and a stocking cap into which tiny bells were sewn. They jingled to his light, prancing steps.

Wamba carried a make-believe wooden sword in his belt. The little sword seemed to make fun of a world ruled by kings, princes and knights in armor with frightening swords and battle-axes of iron.

As they made their way, Gurth spoke. "Since William and his cruel Normans took this land from us, we have known nothing but trouble."

"Yes, my friend, and matters are worse with good King Richard captured by his enemies on his way home from the Crusade. He's in an Austrian prison. His brother, Prince John, rules in Richard's name, but he's no friend to Saxons. His Norman followers rob from us and throw us off our lands. Even our good master Cedric must soon fall to them."

As they spoke, men on horses came near to them. "I am Prior Aymer of Jourvaulx Abbey. We seek lodging for the night. Please direct us to Rotherwood."

"Be quick about it," roared a knight in armor, riding at Prior Aymer's side. "We have no time to waste on Saxon servants."

Gurth grew red in the face. His hand slid to the handle of his knife. "Now, what if we refuse?" he growled.

"Saxon dog. I'll split you open," said the knight, reaching to undo his great, broad sword.

"Now, now," said Prior Aymer, "here are a few coins for good directions, my children."

"Along this path, an hour's ride, you will come to a fork at the large oak tree. Take the left fork and in another hour you will be at Rotherwood," said Wamba. At that, the party of Normans rode off.

"Well done," laughed Gurth. "The left fork will put them deep in the bog. They'll be tramping around all night. Ho, Ho on you, knight in rattling armor."

Coming to the fork, the party of Normans found a pilgrim resting beneath the great oak tree. He was wrapped around in a long, gray, woolen cloak. A walking stick lay at his side. A large cross hung at his chest. A wide hat cast a shadow hiding his face.

"I am Brian de Bois Guilbert, Knight of the Holy Templar. We seek lodging at Rotherwood. Shall we take the left or right fork?"

"By all means, the right fork. The left leads to a bog. I will lead you there, for that's where I'm going tonight," said the pilgrim.

At Rotherwood, Cedric, in his dining hall, scowled at the thought of feeding Normans. But by custom, he had to. Cedric was a strong, handsome man of 60 years. Blue eyes blazed in a wide face beneath a head of thick, blond hair that fell to his shoulders.

The Norman party entered the great dining hall and took their places at the table. Lady Rowena was last to enter. She was a Saxon princess with blond hair and green eyes. Cedric was her protector.

The lord of Rotherwood was a fiery man. He and his guests soon began arguing over the courage and skills of Saxon and Norman warriors.

As tempers flared, Isaac of York, a Jewish merchant said to have great, but secret, wealth, entered the hall seeking lodging for the night. Because Jews of the time were badly treated, Isaac entered with fear. He was an older man with gray hair and a beard framing a narrow, handsome face.

Bois Guilbert shouted loudly at the frightened old man, saying he would not eat at the same table with Isaac.

"Then you will leave this hall and go hungry, Knight Templar," said Cedric. "Any man who comes in peace, whether he be Christian, Jew, or Moslem, is welcome at my table."

Bois Guilbert fell back into his seat grumbling, and busied himself eating.

The quarrel soon started again. As Bois Guilbert boasted of the courage of Norman knights in the Crusade, the pilgrim stood and spoke.

"You talk bravely here, Sir Knight, but in the tournament you and your knights lost to King Richard and a band of Saxon knights."

"A loose strap, pilgrim, and a well-aimed lance by one called Ivanhoe caused me to fall from my horse. But he'll meet his end at the point of my lance if he dares meet me again."

"I'll accept that challenge for him," said the pilgrim.

"And I give my word that Ivanhoe will meet you in tournament," Rowena said, shocking all. For Ivanhoe was the title of Wilfred, Cedric's son. Wilfred was Rowena's true love.

But Cedric would not recognize Wilfred as his son. Wilfred had pledged loyalty to Richard, the Norman king. And he fought at his side in the Crusade.

As the meal ended, Bois Guilbert found Isaac. "Watch out, merchant," he hissed.

Leaving, the pilgrim heard Bois Guilbert speaking to his guards. They would seize Isaac on the road the next day and steal his gold.

Saxon Meets Norman

COMPREHENSION CHECK

Choose the best answer.

1. Good King Richard was captured by his enemies on his way home from
   ___a. Jourvaulx Abbey.
   ___b. Rotherwood.
   ___c. an Austrian prison.
   ___d. the Crusade.

2. While Richard was away in prison, who ruled the land?
   ___a. Cedric of Rotherwood
   ___b. Wamba, the jester
   ___c. Prince John
   ___d. Prior Aymer

3. Prince John was very cruel to
   ___a. the Saxons.
   ___b. the Normans.
   ___c. Brian de Bois Guilbert.
   ___d. all the Knights Templar.

4. Prior Aymer and his fellow Normans came upon Gurth and Wamba and asked directions to Rotherwood. Then, Wamba gave them directions that would lead them to the bog. Next, the party of Normans came upon
   ___a. Cedric of Rotherwood.
   ___b. a pilgrim resting beneath a great oak tree.
   ___c. Isaac of York.
   ___d. King Richard.

5. Wamba had given the Normans the wrong directions because
   ___a. he didn't know the way.
   ___b. he liked to play tricks on people.
   ___c. he didn't like the Normans.
   ___d. he did not get along with Prior Aymer.

6. At the great dining hall at Rotherwood, Bois Guilbert said he would not
   ___a. eat at the same table with Isaac.
   ___b. eat at the same table with Saxons.
   ___c. sit next to Lady Rowena.
   ___d. sit next to Cedric.

7. Jews of the time were treated
   ___a. with respect.
   ___b. kindly.
   ___c. badly.
   ___d. like children.

8. Lady Rowena promised Bois Guilbert that Ivanhoe would
   ___a. split him open.
   ___b. challenge him in the tournament.
   ___c. become King of England one day.
   ___d. put him in prison.

9. Another name for this story could be
   ___a. "The Cruel Rule of Prince John."
   ___b. "Dinner at Rotherwood."
   ___c. "Rowena's Love for Ivanhoe."
   ___d. "The Great Wealth of Isaac of York."

10. This story is mainly about
    ___a. the poor way the Normans treated the Saxons.
    ___b. Cedric's love for Isaac.
    ___c. Rowena's love for Ivanhoe.
    ___d. Bois Guilbert's plan to steal Isaac's gold.

Check your answers with the key on page 67.

Saxon Meets Norman

VOCABULARY CHECK

armor	blond	bog	cloak	merchant	tournament

I. Sentences to Finish

Fill in the blank in each sentence with the correct key word from the box above.

1. Our dog, Foo-Foo has long, _____ hair.

2. The _____ closed his store each night at six o'clock.

3. The tennis _____ will last for several days.

4. While walking to school, Jim slipped in the _____ and dirtied his clothes.

5. The knight's _____ will protect him from the sword's sharp blade.

6. The prince wore a _____ of deep purple.

II. Find the right words and put a check next to the correct answer.

1. Cedric of Rotherwood had long hair that fell to his shoulders. What color was his hair?
   _____ a. Blue _____ b. Brown _____ c. Blond _____ d. Black

2. Isaac of York was a
   _____ a. magician. _____ b. manager. _____ c. messenger. _____ d. merchant.

3. Wamba gave the Normans directions that would lead them to the
   _____ a. bog. _____ b. bank. _____ c. barn. _____ d. beach.

4. The pilgrim resting beneath the oak tree wore a long, gray, woolen
   _____ a. coat. _____ b. cloak. _____ c. cap. _____ d. carpet.

5. Brave knights in days of old would fight each other in
   _____ a. trousers. _____ b. tar. _____ c. tournament. _____ d. tents.

6. When knights fought in tournament, what did they wear to protect themselves?
   _____ a. Armor _____ b. Acorns _____ c. Alarms _____ d. Anchors

Check your answers with the key on page 69.

VICTORY TO AN UNKNOWN KNIGHT

PREPARATION

Key Words

defeat	(di fēt´)	to win victory over; beat *Baseball fans are happy to see their team <u>defeat</u> the other team.*
helmet	(hel´ mit)	a piece of armor, usually of metal, used to protect the head *You should wear a <u>helmet</u> when riding a bicycle.*
mighty	(mī´ te)	having or showing great power, strength or force *The <u>mighty</u> giant scared all the children.*
shield	(shēld)	1. a piece of armor made of leather, metal or wood that is carried on the forearm to protect the body from a blow or strike *He held his <u>shield</u> high to protect his face from the arrows.* 2. protect *A bear will do anything to <u>shield</u> her cubs from harm.*
thrust	(thrust)	to push or drive quickly with force *The <u>thrust</u> of the lance knocked the knight from his horse.*
yelp	(yelp)	the quick sharp bark or cry of a dog, fox, etc. *We heard the <u>yelp</u> of a frightened puppy.*

VICTORY TO AN UNKNOWN KNIGHT

Necessary Words

jousting   (joust´ing)   fighting with lances between two mounted knights
In days of old, <u>jousting</u> was a popular sport.

noble   (nō´ bl)   a person great by birth, rank or title
The <u>noble</u> man was made a knight by the king.

Places

England   is a country in Europe.

Ashby   is a town in England.

Sheffield   is a town in England.

Leicester   is a town in England.

VICTORY TO AN UNKNOWN KNIGHT

"Ivanhoe is well enough, but I don't know when he'll return to England," the pilgrim lied.

Preview:
1. Read the name of the story.
2. Look at the picture.
3. Read the sentence under the picture.
4. Read the first three paragraphs of the story.
5. Then answer the following question.

You learned from your preview that the pilgrim pledged to keep his disguise until
___ a. Rowena married him.
___ b. he left England.
___ c. King Richard showed his face in England.
___ d. Prince John asked to see his face.

Turn to the Comprehension Check on page 16 for the right answer.

Now read the story.

Read to find out who is defeated on the first day of the tournament at Ashby.

#
VICTORY TO AN UNKNOWN KNIGHT

After the meal, Rowena sent for the pilgrim. She wanted further news of Ivanhoe.

"He is well enough," said the pilgrim, lowering his voice and lowering his hat over his face, "but I don't know when he'll be in England."

This was a white lie. For in front of her, in pilgrim's clothes, was, in fact, Ivanhoe himself. He had pledged to keep his disguise until King Richard showed his face in England. Richard had been out of the country too long. Were his Norman nobles still loyal? Or were they siding with Prince John who wanted Richard's throne? Before showing his face, Richard would have to find out.

Even as Rowena and the pilgrim spoke, knights from across England were traveling to the town of Ashby. A great tournament was to be held there in three days. Prince John himself would attend, and he would be looking for loyal followers.

"If only Ivanhoe could be at Ashby to challenge Bois Guilbert and defeat him," sighed Rowena.

"Yes. A Saxon un-horsing the best of the mighty Norman knights in front of Prince John might stop these Normans until Richard arrives," said the pilgrim in his disguised voice.

When he left Rowena, the pilgrim found Isaac asleep. He woke the old man and warned him of Bois Guilbert's plan to rob him.

"You must help me, pilgrim. Help me escape these evil men," wailed Isaac.

The pilgrim found Gurth, the herdsman, his boyhood friend, at Rotherwood. This once he shared his secret and let Gurth know he was Wilfred of Ivanhoe. Gurth gave a yelp of joy. He would do anything for his old friend, his master's son. Gurth found horses for Isaac and Ivanhoe. The two were away and on the road before sunrise.

At mid-morning, Isaac and the pilgrim came to a hill above Sheffield, a town where Isaac had business. Danger was behind them.

"Farewell, Isaac, and take care."

"Wait, pilgrim. These old eyes and ears tell me you are not simply a pilgrim. Your kindness and courage tell me that, too. Beneath those gray clothes, I suspect there may be a good and true knight. One, I should guess, who would happily bear arms against Bois Guilbert at Ashby."

"You surprise me, old man. But, as you can see, I am without war horse and armor."

Isaac took paper and a pen from a flat box he carried with him. He laid the paper on the box and wrote carefully. When he finished, he folded the paper and gave it to the pilgrim.

"Go into the town of Leicester and give this letter to a merchant named Jairam (jy-ram). He owes me favors. He will arrange horse and armor for you to do battle at Ashby. Farewell, Sir Knight," said Isaac, as they parted.

Crowds of people streamed into Ashby. Knights gathered at either end of the long tournament field. Colorful banners and flags fluttered in the breeze. Excitement was in the air. Prince John and his followers entered the royal box. In the stands, across from the royal box, sat Cedric and the Saxons. Rowena was there, too. So was Athelstane, great, great grandson of Harold, the last Saxon king of England.

A band of Saxons all dressed in the green of the forest sat in the stands. Shouting and name-calling started. Isaac and his beautiful daughter Rebecca had entered the stands. Isaac was there for two reasons. Prince John ordered him to be there. Isaac was a money lender, and Prince John needed money to carry out his plan to take Richard's throne. But besides, Isaac wanted to see the pilgrim knight defeat Bois Guilbert.

Bois Guilbert, in full armor, sat on his horse with lance and shield. At Prince John's command, trumpets sounded to begin the jousting. The Knight Templar and a knight at the other end of the field drove their horses in a gallop toward one another. Bois Guilbert's lance struck a mighty blow on his challenger's shield, un-horsing him.

Through the morning, Bois Guilbert and his fellow knights defeated all challengers. By early afternoon there seemed none left to challenge. Prince was about to call an end to the jousting and declare Bois Guilbert champion. Suddenly, a knight in dark blue armor on a coal-black horse appeared at the far end of the field. His helmet hid his face. He refused to give his name. He had pledged to remain unknown, he said.

He called out a challenge to Bois Guilbert. He challenged each of Bois Guilbert's companions as well. The stands came alive with wild cheering, for never had such a challenge been made. England's five champion knights had been targeted by an unknown knight.

First it was Bois Guilbert. The Knight Templar and the Unknown Knight came together in a loud crash. Bois Guilbert, taking the thrust of the lance on his shield, just managed to hold his seat. As they came at one another again, the Unknown Knight aimed his lance low at Bois Guilbert's shield. At the last split-second, he thrust the lance high to the helmet. Down with a yelp of surprise went Bois Guilbert like a tree.

One by one, Bois Guilbert's fellow knights tried to un-horse the Unknown Knight. But he was able to shield himself from all blows. Each in turn was soundly knocked from his horse. The cheering in the stands was deafening. But with the defeat of his champion knights, angry Prince John stormed out of the royal box. "Who will pledge loyalty to me now!" he thought.

VICTORY TO AN UNKNOWN KNIGHT

COMPREHENSION CHECK

Choose the best answer.

1. The pilgrim was really
   ___a. King Richard.
   ___b. Ivanhoe.
   ___c. Prince John.
   ___d. Gurth, the herdsman.

2. Rowena
   ___a. was fooled by Ivanhoe's disguise.
   ___b. was not fooled by Ivanhoe's disguise.
   ___c. thought Ivanhoe looked funny in his woolen cloak.
   ___d. was mad that Ivanhoe tried to fool her.

3. The pilgrim shared the secret of who he really was
   ___a. with Rebecca.
   ___b. with Isaac.
   ___c. with Jairam.
   ___d. with Gurth.

4. A great tournament was to be held in the town of
   ___a. Ashbury.
   ___b. Aspen.
   ___c. Ashby.
   ___d. Aster.

5. Who was it that helped Ivanhoe get war horse and armor to do battle at Ashby?
   ___a. Gurth
   ___b. Isaac
   ___c. Rowena
   ___d. King Richard

6. Bois Guilbert
   ___a. was not skilled with a sword.
   ___b. had no horse sense.
   ___c. was one of Prince John's champion knights.
   ___d. was one of King Richard's champion knights.

7. The Unknown Knight who defeated Bois Guilbert and his fellow knights was
   ___a. Ivanhoe.
   ___b. King Richard.
   ___c. Athelstane.
   ___d. Cedric of Rotherwood.

8. The defeat of his champion knights
   ___a. pleased Prince John.
   ___b. angered Prince John.
   ___c. made the prince cry.
   ___d. made the prince laugh.

9. Another name for this story could be
   ___a. "Isaac's Kindness."
   ___b. "Bois Guilbert's Big Win."
   ___c. "Prince John's Loyal Followers."
   ___d. "Ivanhoe's Success at Ashby."

10. This story is mainly about
    ___a. how Prince John's plan to win new followers was spoiled by Ivanhoe's victory.
    ___b. Rowena's plan to find Ivanhoe.
    ___c. Isaac's fear of Bois Guilbert and his men.
    ___d. Isaac, the money lender.

Check your answers with the key on page 67.

This page may be reproduced for classroom use.

VICTORY TO AN UNKNOWN KNIGHT

VOCABULARY CHECK

defeat	helmet	mighty	shield	thrust	yelp

I. Sentences to Finish

Fill in the blank in each sentence with the correct key word from the box above.

1. Sam wondered if he could _____ the winner of last year's race.

2. I heard the _____ of an animal deep in the forest.

3. When a robber entered the house, Sally quickly _____ her money under the rug.

4. The _____ force of the storm knocked down the tree.

5. During battle, a _____ is worn to protect one's head.

6. The soldier held up his _____ to protect his body.

II. Use the blank spaces to write the words that do not belong.

1 Which word does <u>not</u> belong with defeat?
   a. beat   b. win   c. surrender   _____

2. Which word does <u>not</u> belong with helmet?
   a. metal   b. head   c. wrinkle   _____

3. Which word does <u>not</u> belong with mighty?
   a. patient   b. powerful   c. strong   _____

4. Which word does <u>not</u> belong with shield?
   a. armor   b. coin   c. protect   _____

5. Which word does <u>not</u> belong with thrust?
   a. push   b. shove   c. examine   _____

6. Which word does <u>not</u> belong with yelp?
   a. bark   b. grumble   c. cry

Check your answers with the key on page 69.

Debts are Paid

PREPARATION

Key Words

advise   (ad vīz´)   to inform; notify
> *Ruth will <u>advise</u> me of the time for my next lesson.*

nimble   (nim´ bl)   quick and light in movement or action
> *Mary plays the piano with <u>nimble</u> fingers.*

otherwise   (uTH´ ər wīz)   under other circumstances; or else
> *It rained; <u>otherwise</u> I might have taken a walk.*

purse   (pėrs)   a small bag or pouch for carrying money
> *Mother's <u>purse</u> is always full of change.*

repay   (ri pā´)   to pay back
> *Meg must <u>repay</u> a loan to the bank.*

squire   (skwīr)   a young man who attends (takes care of) a knight until he himself is made a night
(As happened in "Ivanhoe," Gurth, a herdsman, was well above his station as squire.)
> *The knight sent for his <u>squire</u> to bring him a fresh horse.*

Debts are Paid

Necessary Words

People

Locksley   Robert Locksley, better known as Robin Hood. The outlaw who robbed from the rich to give to the poor.

Debts are Paid

As Gurth worried about what Cedric would do to him if he was caught, four squires approached the tent.

Preview:
1. Read the name of the story.
2. Look at the picture.
3. Read the sentence under the picture.
4. Read the first two paragraphs of the story.
5. Then answer the following question.

You learned from your preview that Gurth became a squire to
___ a. Cedric.
___ b. the Unknown Knight.
___ c. Bois Guilbert.
___ d. Prince John.

Turn to the Comprehension Check on page 22 for the right answer.

Now read the story.

Read to find out who Gurth meets as he makes his way back to his master.

Debts are Paid

No longer one of Cedric's herdsmen, Gurth the herdsman stood outside the blue-and-white tent in the camp of the knights. The pilgrim, Wilfred of Ivanhoe in disguise, had need of his services. And so Gurth became squire to the Unknown Knight. "Heaven help me," he thought, "when Cedric catches up with me." For Gurth had left Rotherwood without telling a soul, the minute his new master called.

As Gurth thought of these things, four squires approached the tent. They were leading large war horses. A suit of armor was strapped to the saddle of each horse. It was the custom for a defeated knight to surrender horse and armor to the winning knight.

Gurth announced the squires' arrival, and the Unknown Knight received them. From each he accepted ransom money instead of horse and armor, which is also the custom. But not from Bois Guilbert's squire.

"Advise your master," said the Unknown Knight, "that it is not ended between us. Advise him to keep horse and armor. He will soon need them because when we meet again we will fight to the death."

When the squires left, the Unknown Knight sent for Gurth. Out of the ransom he took a sum to repay Isaac for his own horse and armor. Gurth took the gold and went on his way.

In Ashby, Gurth found Isaac staying at a friend's house and made the payment. Then a strange thing happened. As he was leaving, Gurth was called aside by Rebecca, Isaac's daughter.

"Squire, how much did your master give you to repay my father for horse and armor?"

"Eighty gold pieces," answered Gurth.

Rebecca handed Gurth a silk purse. "There are 100 gold pieces here. Return the 80 to your master and keep 20 for yourself, squire. It is a small price for seeing my father away safely from Rotherwood."

Gurth couldn't have been more surprised or pleased as he made his way back to his master through the woods. A couple of more days like this, he thought, and I'll be able to buy my freedom from Cedric. Then, as he passed a large oak tree, two men jumped out in the path in front of him, and two others behind him.

"These woods are dangerous at night, friend. Robbers would cut your throat for a penny," said one.

"What's in your pockets? We'll protect you," said another.

"I need no man to protect me. If you'll step out of the way, I'll pass," said Gurth.

Before he could take a step, the four men were on him. They knocked Gurth to the ground and held him while one went through his clothing and found the purses.

"What have we here? Why, it looks like gold. And quite a bit of it!"

Gurth was lifted to his feet and marched through the woods. They came to a clearing where a large group of men stood around.

"We found this fellow and what do you think he was carrying?" said one of Gurth's captors, holding out his and Rebecca's purses.

"Well now, my man. Who are you and what are you doing with all this money?" asked a tall man coming forward.

Gurth recognized him as their leader. He sat with these men in the stands behind Cedric at the tournament. All were dressed in forest green.

"The gold belongs to my master, the Unknown Knight," said Gurth, angrily. "And if you are good Saxons, you'll not take it."

"Well, well, you are bold," said the leader. "And we do admire the knight greatly for tumbling the Normans. But if he lets a fellow like you hold his gold on the road at night, it might mean that you are able to protect it. Otherwise, if you really are not fit to protect it, the good knight should know."

The leader spoke to one of his men. He was a miller, a man who grinds wheat into flour as his trade. He was Gurth's size, but stronger. He carried a quarter-staff, a five-foot length of hardwood, round, thick and strong. It was a weapon used for protection and in sporting contests by the common people.

"You, miller, will defend the honor of our band of men against the squire. And squire, if you can knock over the miller like your master knocked over the Normans today, you can leave with your gold," spoke the leader. "Otherwise, we'll hold the gold for safety and bring it and you back to the good knight — like a little boy who shouldn't be out alone at night."

Gurth snorted. He was given a quarter-staff, and he and the miller faced each other in a tight circle. They struck out with fury as quarter-staff landed on quarter-staff with sharp cracks — on shoulders, arms and ribs. The miller was the stronger, but Gurth was more nimble. He dodged more blows and struck more blows. The miller grew tired and Gurth saw his chance. He aimed a blow to the miller's left side. When the miller shifted his quarter-staff to catch the blow, Gurth, with lightning speed, yanked back his staff and sent it up with great force to the side of the miller's head. Down went the miller.

"Well done, nimble squire," said the leader, as he helped the groggy miller to his feet. "Keep your gold and go in peace. Tell your master that Locksley and his men would be proud to fight at his side against our Norman enemies if ever he needs us."

Debts are Paid

COMPREHENSION CHECK

Choose the best answer.

1. By custom, what was a defeated knight supposed to surrender to the winner?
   ___a. His sword
   ___b. His helmet
   ___c. His war horse and armor, or money
   ___d. His silver and gold

2. The Unknown Knight
   ___a. did not like Bois Guilbert.
   ___b. loved Bois Guilbert.
   ___c. liked Bois Guilbert like a brother.
   ___d. was Bois Guilbert's closest friend.

3. Out of the ransom, the Unknown Knight gave Gurth a sum to
   ___a. buy a better horse.
   ___b. buy a sharper sword.
   ___c. repay Isaac for his horse and armor.
   ___d. repay Isaac for his kindness.

4. First, the Unknown Knight gave Gurth 80 gold pieces to repay Isaac. Then, Gurth found Isaac and made the payment. Next,
   ___a. Gurth returned to his master.
   ___b. he was jumped by a gang in the woods.
   ___c. Rebecca thanked him.
   ___d. Rebecca returned the payment and gave Gurth 20 coins for himself.

5. Why did Rebecca return the payment?
   ___a. She didn't like accepting money from anyone.
   ___b. Her father was rich and didn't need the money.
   ___c. It was her way of telling the Unknown Knight "Thank You" for helping her father.
   ___d. She knew that the Unknown Knight needed the money.

6. When Rebecca told Gurth to keep 20 coins for himself,
   ___a. he became upset.
   ___b. he was very pleased.
   ___c. he was not thankful.
   ___d. he mumbled to himself.

7. Who were the men who stopped Gurth in the woods as he was returning to his master?
   ___a. Robin Hood and his men
   ___b. Bois Guilbert and his men
   ___c. Prince John and his Norman followers
   ___d. the Knights Templar

8. If Gurth was to keep his master's gold he had to
   ___a. fight Locksley to the death.
   ___b. fight Cedric.
   ___c. defeat the miller.
   ___d. defeat Locksley's men, one by one.

9. Another name for this story could be
   ___a. "Gurth Gets Rich."
   ___b. "Gurth Protects his Master's Gold."
   ___c. "Gurth Buys his Freedom."
   ___d. "Isaac's Rich Daughter."

10. This story is mainly about
    ___a. how Gurth got rich in Ashby.
    ___b. the Unknown Knight's threat to Bois Guilbert.
    ___c. Rebecca's kindness to a poor squire.
    ___d. how Gurth protects and defends his new master.

Check your answers with the key on page 67.

Debts are Paid

VOCABULARY CHECK

advise	nimble	otherwise	purse	repay	squire

I. Sentences to Finish

Fill in the blank in each sentence with the correct key word from the box above.

1. I will _____ my friends that I will be giving a party on Saturday.

2. The _____ worked very hard to please his new master.

3. If Bob asks me nicely, I will help him paint the fence; _____ he can do it himself.

4. Mother left her leather _____ on the grocery counter.

5. Jack said I can borrow ten dollars if I _____ him on Friday.

6. The musician played the guitar with _____ fingers.

II. Word Search

All the words in the box above are hidden in the puzzle below. They may be written from left to right, or up and down. As you find each word, draw a circle around it. One word, that is not a key word, has been done for you.

```
M  N  I  M  S  Q  O  J  A  R
A  D  V  I  N  E  T  B  L  E
E  R  E  P  A  L  H  N  I  M
O  T  H  E  R  R  E  P  A  Y
N  I  M  B  P  U  R  S  E  X
B  N  I  M  L  L  W  S  Q  R
S  A  R  P  U  R  I  R  U  P
Q  D  E  G  N  O  S  O  T  H
U  S  Q  U  I  R  E  P  A  Y
A  D  V  I  M  W  O  A  D  V
N  I  M  L  B  C  T  Y  V  S
B  L  I  M  L  U  H  D  I  P
X  C  U  R  E  P  E  R  S  A
L  A  U  M  O  T  N  W  E  W
```

Check your answers with the key on page 69.

This page may be reproduced for classroom use.

A Champion is Wounded

PREPARATION

Key Words

mercy	(mur´ sē)	kind treatment of a person *The town shelter where the homeless are given a meal and a bed for the night is a house of <u>mercy</u>.*
severe	(sə vir´)	hard or sharp *A <u>severe</u> gust of wind blew the flowerpot through the window.*
slash	(slash)	a cut or other injury *The <u>slash</u> on the palm of his hand required stitching.*
sunk	(sungk)	having gone down slowly *The ship <u>sunk</u> lower and lower into the water after hitting the iceberg.*
thrown	(thrōn)	to be hurled to the ground *After being <u>thrown</u> off the horse, I decided to take riding lessons.*
vicious	(vish´ əs)	dangerous; evil; wicked *A <u>vicious</u> man-eating shark circled the lifeboat.*

A Champion is Wounded

Necessary Words

herald   (her´əld)   a person who carries messages and makes announcements

> *The <u>herald</u> sounded his trumpet for the tournament to begin.*

People

Athelstane   is a Saxon knight.

A Champion is Wounded

The tournament about to begin, Prince John and his court wait anxiously in the royal box.

Preview:
1. Read the name of the story.
2. Look at the picture.
3. Read the sentence under the picture.
4. Read the first two paragraphs of the story.
5. Then answer the following question.

You learned from your preview that group jousting was
___ a. more dangerous than one knight jousting with another.
___ b. a sport that required no skill.
___ c. an easy sport to learn.
___ d. a sport that was of interest to no one.

Turn to the Comprehension Check on page 28 for the right answer.

Now read the story.

Read to find out what happens to Prince John's champion knight.

A Champion is Wounded

A great clatter swept over the field on the second day of the tournament. Knights and heralds on horses hurried to their positions. Dust swirled up from the horses' feet. It dimmed the bright yellows and golds, purples, blues, greens and reds of the coverings and costumes of horse and man. The viewing stands quickly filled. Prince John and his court seated themselves in the royal box.

At either end of the field, some 50 knights gathered to join in group jousting. They would fight side-by-side against their opposite numbers. Group jousting required less skill, but was dangerous. More so than one knight jousting with another.

At one end, knights were gathering to the banner of their champion, Brian de Bois Guilbert. At the other end, to the banner of the Unknown Knight. Curiously, Athelstane, of the royal Saxon blood, chose to join Bois Guilbert. This surprised and angered Cedric, his fellow Saxon, who had no use for the Norman conquerors. It seemed Athelstane was angered that the Unknown Knight - declared champion on the first day - had chosen Rowena as First Lady of the tournament. It was expected that Athelstane and Rowena, both of royal Saxon blood, would one day marry. Who was this Unknown Knight that he should claim Rowena as his First Lady? Mighty Athelstane would deal him a severe blow today if they met.

Placing himself in the middle of the first line, Bois Guilbert formed two lines each of 25 knights, one behind the other. At the other end of the field the Unknown Knight arranged his knights in the same manner. Horses snorted and pawed at the earth, reined in by their riders whose lances pointed skyward. At the sound of the heralds' trumpets, the first lines lowered their lances and charged. The lines met in a vicious clash of lance and shield, armor and horse and shriek of horse and man.

"Show them no mercy," cried the warriors.

Great balls of dust rose up and hid the scene for the moment. As the dust faded, clearly half the number of knights had been thrown from their horses. Some lay still on the ground. Some struggled to their feet with sword or battle-ax to fight on foot. Some were wounded and being helped from the field. Knights still on horse held broken lances and were reaching for other weapons. They were joined by knights coming up from the second line, and the battle continued.

Bois Guilbert and the Unknown Knight could not find one another in the crowding. But as knights fell and the numbers on the field grew fewer, they soon found their way to one another. Bois Guilbert's horse bled from a deep sword slash and was not carrying him well. The Unknown Knight on his strong black stallion attacked. Just as he was ready to unhorse the Knight Templar, two huge knights came to Bois Guilbert's rescue. One was Athelstane, coming in from the right. And from the left came Reginald Front-de-Boeuf, a most feared and vicious Norman knight.

The three now attacked the Unknown Knight. Before long, one would certainly cut him down. Yet he wheeled his great horse this way and that and slashed out at his enemies with such great strength and speed, that he had them backing away. Soon, though, he grew tired and his enemies surrounded him. Front-de-Boeuf saw his chance and raised his great sword, aiming a slash at the unprotected neck. As the sword came forward, it was knocked from his hand with a great clang.

A tall knight in black armor on a large black stallion brought his sword down a second time: on Front-de-Boeuf's helmet, knocking the knight to the ground. The Black Knight now circled behind the Unknown Knight. He came alongside Athelstane and yanked the battle-ax from his hand, as if taking candy from a baby. With the flat of the ax he struck the surprised Athelstane a severe blow to his helmet

and he, too, was thrown from his horse. Then the Black Knight left the fighting to the Knight Templar and the Unknown Knight.

On the wounded horse, Bois Guilbert was no match for his enemy. His horse now staggered badly. The Unknown Knight brought his sword forward in a mighty overhead swing. Bois Guilbert rose up with his shield to meet the blow while yanking on the reins to turn the horse aside. The poor beast sunk to its knees, and his rider tumbled in the dirt. Prince John, seeing his champion, Bois Guilbert, on the ground at the mercy of the Unknown Knight, quickly called a halt to the contest.

The prince was ready to name the Black Knight champion, but that knight could nowhere be found. Scowling, he was forced, once again, to name the Unknown Knight champion of the day.

A weary champion rode slowly to the royal box. Once again, he refused to remove his helmet. Then, as the crowned unknown champion turned from the royal box, he sunk in his saddle and slid from his horse to the ground. Blood ran from a wound in his side; he did not move. The prince's servants moved quickly to help him and removed the helmet he himself would not remove. His eyes were closed. What shocked all, including Prince John, was the familiar face. It was the face of Wilfred of Ivanhoe! Like wild fire, word raced through the crowds that the Unknown Knight was Ivanhoe. Prince John frowned. A faithful warrior of his brother, King Richard, was in England! Trembling, the prince wondered, "Could Richard be here, too?"

A Champion is Wounded

COMPREHENSION CHECK

Choose the best answer.

1. Athelstane
   ___a. was Prince John's brother.
   ___b. was a Norman knight.
   ___c. was of royal Saxon blood.
   ___d. was Bois Guilbert's best friend.

2. Cedric, Saxon lord of Rotherwood, was angered to learn that Athelstane
   ___a. gathered to the banner of Bois Guilbert.
   ___b. gathered to the banner of the Unknown Knight.
   ___c. did not want to attend the tournament.
   ___d. left the tournament early.

3. Athelstane was angry that the Unknown Knight
   ___a. was declared champion on the first day of the tournament.
   ___b. would not show his face.
   ___c. wanted to marry Rowena.
   ___d. had chosen Rowena as First Lady of the tournament.

4. It had been expected that, one day,
   ___a. Bois Guilbert would marry Rowena.
   ___b. Athelstane and Rowena would marry.
   ___c. Athelstane would be a tournament champion.
   ___d. Athelstane would become king.

5. Who came to Bois Guilbert's rescue just as the Unknown Knight was about to unhorse him?
   ___a. Prince John
   ___b. Athelstane
   ___c. Front-de-Boeuf
   ___d. Athelstane and Front-de-Boeuf

6. Who came to the Unknown Knight's rescue, just as Front-de-Boeuf prepared to slash his neck?
   ___a. A tall knight in black armor
   ___b. A small knight on a black horse
   ___c. Cedric of Rotherwood
   ___d. Lady Rowena

7. The Unknown Knight was declared champion once again, but not before being wounded
   ___a. in the neck.
   ___b. in the back.
   ___c. in his side.
   ___d. in the head.

8. Why did Prince John tremble when he thought that his brother might be in England?
   ___a. He owed his brother money.
   ___b. His brother hated him.
   ___c. Since his brother was king, Prince John would no longer rule England.
   ___d. He trembled with joy at the thought of seeing his brother again.

9. Another name for this story could be
   ___a. "Ivanhoe, the Wounded Knight."
   ___b. "Prince John Frowns at Ivanhoe."
   ___c. "King Richard Returns."
   ___d. "A Weary Champion."

10. This story is mainly about
    ___a. Prince John's love for King Richard.
    ___b. Athelstane's love for Rowena.
    ___c. the Unknown Knight's jousting skills.
    ___d. how the Unknown Knight is discovered to be Wilfred of Ivanhoe.

Check your answers with the key on page 67.

This page may be reproduced for classroom use.

A Champion is Wounded

VOCABULARY CHECK

mercy	severe	slash	sunk	thrown	vicious

I. Sentences to Finish

Fill in the blank in each sentence with the correct key word from the box above.

1. A _____ blow to his stomach sent the fighter to his knees.

2. The penny _____ to the bottom of the wishing well.

3. Sally has _____ away all her old dolls.

4. The policeman will _____ the thief's tires so he can't get away.

5. Hungry wolves are _____ animals.

6. The thief begged the judge for _____ .

II. Mixed-up Words

First, unscramble the letters in Column A to spell out the key words. Then, match the key words with the right meaning in Column B by drawing a line.

Column A	Column B
1. worthn _____	a. dangerous; evil; wicked
2. cryme _____	b. having gone down slowly
3. halss _____	c. to be hurled to the ground
4. sciouvi _____	d. kind treatment of a person
5. nuks _____	e. hard or sharp
6. everes _____	f. a cut or other injury

Check your answers with the key on page 70.

This page may be reproduced for classroom use.

Bad News for Prince John

PREPARATION

Key Words

attend	(ə tend´)	1. to take care of (a sick person, for example); wait on
		    The nurse will <u>attend</u> to your sick mother.
		2. be present at
		    We will <u>attend</u> the school play.

delay	(di lā´)	put off until a later time *We will not <u>delay</u> the party because of the bad weather.*
heal	(hēl)	to cure *The doctor is waiting for my cut to <u>heal</u>.*
release	(ri lēs´)	to set free *Joe opened the cage to <u>release</u> the bird.*
separate	(sep´ ə rit)	set apart from others *The twins are now in <u>separate</u> classrooms.*
splendid	(splen´ did)	grand; fine; excellent *Kate brought home a <u>splendid</u> report card.*

Bad News for Prince John

Necessary Words

art   (ärt)   a special skill
Joe's dad taught him the <u>art</u> of kite flying.

dungeon   (dun´ jən)   a dark, underground cell used to hold prisoners
The man was sent to the <u>dungeon</u> for his crime.

outlaw   (out´ lô´)   a criminal
The <u>outlaw</u> was sent to jail for robbing the bank.

yeoman   (yō´ mən)   an independent farmer long ago in England
The <u>yeoman</u> raised many sheep on his land.

People

Maurice de Bracy   is a knight with a small company of soldiers hired by Prince John.

Places

York   is a city in England.

Bad News for Prince John

"I will heal him," Rebecca told her servants. *"Carry him to our house without delay!"*

Preview: 1. Read the name of the story.
                  2. Look at the picture.
                  3. Read the sentences under the picture.
                  4. Read the first five paragraphs of the story.
                  5. Then answer the following question.

You learned from your preview that Rebecca had learned the art of
___ a. jousting.
___ b. cooking.
___ c. healing.
___ d. managing money.

Turn to the Comprehension Check on page 34 for the right answer.

Now read the story.

Read to find out what becomes of the Unknown Knight.

Bad News for Prince John

Word that his son was the Unknown Knight reached Cedric's ears as he rose to leave the stands.

"Hurry. Attend to him at once," he told his servants.

But Rebecca, also in the stands, sent her servants when the knight had first fallen.

"I will heal him. Carry him to our house," she had said. "Do not delay."

Rebecca had learned the art of healing from Miriam, a famous healer among her people. But people had said that Miriam was a witch, and she had been burned at the stake. Fearing what happened to Miriam, Rebecca healed in secret.

In the excitement, Rebecca's servants quietly carried Ivanhoe off on a cot.

"He is being well cared for," Cedric's servants reported back.

Nor was Prince John kept wondering about Richard. A messenger arrived. The prince read the message and turned white.

"Richard gained his release from prison. He is back in England," he snarled.

"We must not delay our plans," said Waldemar Fitzurse, a close friend of the prince. "Our friends are ready to meet in York in three days."

"We need money to raise an army," said Prince John. "Tell Isaac that I will need two thousand gold pieces in York by week's end. If he values his neck!"

As the prince and his court made their way through the crowds, who would have dreamed that two of his closest followers, then riding with him, would be the ruin of his plans?

Bois Guilbert had caught sight of the face of the beautiful Rebecca in the stands. He longed for her from that moment on. Maurice de Bracy thought Lady Rowena most beautiful. But her royal blood and the splendid riches she would bring as a bride was mostly on his mind. With the help of Bois Guilbert, he would try to make Rowena his bride.

Meanwhile, Rebecca was attending to Ivanhoe's wounds. "He is very ill,

Father, but I can heal him."

"Rebecca, we must leave for York. I must gather the money the prince is demanding or it will mean my life. We must leave the knight in the care of others," said Isaac.

"No, Father. We will take him with us, otherwise he will surely die."

Isaac gave in. He hired cot carriers and guards for the journey, and they set off for York.

Cedric, too, prepared to leave Ashby. Then Gurth, his run-away servant, fell into his hands. Oswald, Cedric's guard, had found Gurth looking for his fallen master and brought him to Cedric.

"Tie him up. Put a rope around his neck and drag him along behind us," ordered Cedric, as he led his small party home to Rotherwood.

Now, De Bracy knew Rowena left Ashby in Cedric's party. He would dress his men as outlaws. They would attack Cedric's party when it reached Sherwood Forest. Later, he would appear as himself and "rescue" Rowena. This splendid deed would allow him to ask for her hand.

Cedric and his party found themselves on the same road Isaac had taken earlier. Just as they turned into the forest, they came upon Isaac and his daughter. With them was a cot covered with curtains.

"Good Cedric," cried Isaac, "help us. Let us join you. Fearing outlaws, our guards and carriers ran off."

Cedric agreed and found new carriers. While this was happening, Gurth escaped. Separate from the others, he talked Wamba, his old friend, into cutting him loose and slipped quietly away into the woods.

The party traveled on. But soon the road grew narrow and they had to travel in a single line, which could prove dangerous. In fact, it was here that the "outlaws" chose to attack. They fell on Cedric's party before a sword could be drawn, and they were taken prisoners.

"Now you can leave us and return as the lady's rescuer," Bois Guilbert

whispered wickedly.

"I think not," said De Bracy, suspecting the Knight Templar of mischief. "We'll take the prisoners to Torquilstone, Front-de-Boeuf's castle. There, I'll offer to release Rowena if she will marry me."

They set out for the castle. All, except Wamba. He had escaped, and it took him little time finding Gurth, who came running when he heard his shouts.

"Oh, Gurth, what will we do?" asked Wamba, as the two sat on a rock, having not the least idea what they would do.

Then came a rustle in the trees. A yeoman dressed in green and carrying a long bow stepped out. Gurth recognized him as the leader of the outlaws who held him up in the woods outside of Ashby. He was Locksley, or as Gurth now suspected, Robin Hood.

"You said you would help my master when the time came," said Gurth. "I fear he was on the cot being carried in Cedric's party when it was attacked." Garth told him all that had happened.

That night at Torquilstone, Front-de-Boeuf met his guests. Isaac would bring a ransom in gold, he thought, and had him thrown into the dungeon. The others were led to separate rooms. Only De Bracy knew the cot held Ivanhoe, and he put him in the care of servants. He would use the secret of the wounded knight to get his way with the proud and stubborn Rowena, who angrily refused to marry him.

Bad News for Prince John

COMPREHENSION CHECK

Choose the best answer.

1. When Prince John learned that King Richard was back in England
   ___a. he fainted.
   ___b. he quickly made plans to raise an army.
   ___c. he stole money from Isaac.
   ___d. he ran away to York.

2. Isaac prepared to leave for York to
   ___a. get married.
   ___b. find a husband for Rebecca.
   ___c. get a doctor for Ivanhoe.
   ___d. gather the money Prince John had demanded.

3. Rebecca did not want to
   ___a. leave Ashby.
   ___b. go to York.
   ___c. leave Ivanhoe in the care of others.
   ___d. give any money to Prince John.

4. When Gurth was found and brought before Cedric,
   ___a. Cedric had him tied up.
   ___b. Cedric forgave him.
   ___c. Cedric had him thrown into jail.
   ___d. Cedric ordered him put to death.

5. First, Isaac and his party set out for York. Then, Cedric and his party left for Rotherwood. Next,
   ___a. Gurth escaped.
   ___b. they were attacked by De Bracy and his men.
   ___c. Cedric came upon Isaac and his party.
   ___d. they were brought to Front-de-Boeuf's castle.

6. Instead of "rescuing" Rowena as planned, De Bracy decided to
   ___a. take all the prisoners to Torquelstone.
   ___b. forget his plan to marry Rowena.
   ___c. marry Rebecca instead.
   ___d. return to Ashby.

7. When Locksley found Gurth and Wamba in the forest, why did Gurth tell him all that had happened?
   ___a. He was tired of talking to Wamba.
   ___b. He hoped that Locksley would rescue Rowena.
   ___c. He hoped that Locksley would rescue Rebecca.
   ___d. He hoped that Locksley would make good on his promise to help his master.

8. Why did De Bracy think that he could use the secret of the wounded knight to win Rowena's hand?
   ___a. He knew that if the secret got out, Rowena could get into trouble.
   ___b. He knew that if the secret got out, it would mean trouble for Rowena's protector, Cedric.
   ___c. He knew that Fron-de-Boeuf would kill Rowena if he learned the truth.
   ___d. He knew that if the secret got out, it would bring harm to the man Rowena loved.

9. Another name for this story could be
   ___a. "The Rescuers."
   ___b. "A Most Troubled Journey."
   ___c. "Wamba's Escape."
   ___d. "Stubborn Rowena."

10. This story is mainly about
    ___a. De Bracy's feelings for the lovely Rowena.
    ___b. how Rebecca takes care of Ivanhoe.
    ___c. how the good Saxons came to be prisoners at Torquelstone.
    ___d. Bois Guilbert's mischief.

Check your answers with the key on page 67.

This page may be reproduced for classroom use.

Bad News for Prince John

VOCABULARY CHECK

attend	delay	heal	release	separate	splendid

I. Sentences to Finish

Fill in the blank in each sentence with the correct key word from the box above.

1. Tom will _____ cutting the grass until the very last minute.

2. Kathy did a _____ job decorating the cake.

3. My sister and I have _____ bedrooms; hers is upstairs, mine is down-stairs.

4. The thief looked forward to his _____ from prison.

5. Mothers _____ to the needs of their children.

6. The baby's mother tried hard to _____ her sick child.

II. Crossword Puzzle

Use the words from the box above to fill in the puzzle. The meanings below will help you to choose the right words.

Across

1. to set free
2. put off until a later time
3. to take care of; wait on

Down

1. set apart from others
2. grand; fine; excellent
3. to cure

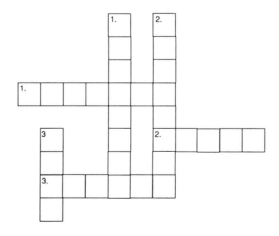

Check your answers with the key on page 70.

This page may be reproduced for classroom use.

A CASTLE FALLS

PREPARATION

Key Words

balcony	(bal´ kə nē)	a platform that projects from the wall of a building and is surrounded by a railing *The only seats we could find were up in the balcony.*
broad	(brôd)	wide from side to side *A bridge was built to get across the broad river.*
clerk	(klẻrk)	Some words lose their meaning over time. In the time of Ivanhoe, a clerk was a church person, a priest, a monk, or friar. Today, a clerk is one who works in an office keeping records or filing letters. A clerk is also one who works in a store as a salesperson. *The sales clerk gave me my change.*
consent	(kən sent´)	to agree *I will not consent to your dating that boy.*
traitor	(trā´ tər)	a person who betrays his country or a cause *Years ago, a traitor would be hanged from a tree.*
twilight	(twī´ līt´)	just after sunset *The fireworks started at twilight.*

A CASTLE FALLS

Necessary Words

friar   (frī´ ər)   a man of the church; a member of a religious order who takes a vow of poverty and supports himself by begging
The <u>friar</u> greeted us as we entered the church.

A CASTLE FALLS

"What I have I'll share with you," spoke the friar, asking the Black Knight to enter.

Preview: 1. Read the name of the story.
2. Look at the picture.
3. Read the sentence under the picture.
4. Read the first five paragraphs of the story.
5. Then answer the following question.

You learned from your preview that the Black Knight, looking for food and shelter, knocked on the door of

___ a. a crumbling church.
___ b. a small hut.
___ c. a schoolhouse.
___ d. a large, handsome castle.

Turn to the Comprehension Check on page 40 for the right answer.

Now read the story.

Read to find out who the Black Knight really is.

A CASTLE FALLS

Twilight came in Sherwood Forest, and a knight on horseback moved out of the woods into a clearing and stopped before a small, crumbling church. It was the Black Knight. With his lance, he knocked loudly on the door of a small hut beside the church.

The door opened and there stood a tall, broad-shouldered friar in a brown wool robe, tied at the waist with a cord.

"Who are you and what do you want?" he growled.

"I'm a knight of honor and I need food and shelter this night. That's all you need to know," said the knight, in a stern voice.

He had the friar's respect. "What I have I'll share with you. Enter."

The friar was the Clerk of Copmanhurst. He lived in the woods, caring for St. Dunstan's Church. But he was also known in the forest as Friar Tuck, one of Robin Hood's outlaws who stole from rich Norman conquerors to give to the poor.

Before long, the two were eating and drinking and singing songs like old friends. This continued into the night until the door shook with a thunderous knock.

"Some clerk you are, singing those songs," came a laughing shout from outside the door.

"Who's ever out there will be finding my quarter-staff on the side of his head!" roared the friar, opening the door. It was Locksley, or Robin Hood, and there was nothing to do but for all to laugh.

"You were at Ivanhoe's side at Ashby, Sir Black Knight," said Locksley, "but I'm afraid he is in more need of your help now." Locksley told him of the attack.

"I'll attend to that traitor Front-de-Boeuf," said the Black Knight.

"They have a head start, but we can travel faster. We have enough men to storm the walls and free the prisoners," boasted Locksley.

Thus, just a few hours after Bois Guilbert, De Bracy, and their prisoners entered Torquilstone, the Black Knight and Locksley and his men came out of the forest and surrounded the castle.

None too soon! Front-de-Boeuf had Isaac stripped of his clothes and the jailers were about to lay him on a rack over red-hot coals. This evil man demanded one thousand pounds of silver - a fortune - as ransom. Isaac would not consent unless his daughter and the others were also released. He was just about to suffer a horrible death, when from outside the castle was heard the loud blast of a hunting horn.

"Leave him be. We'll do this later," said Front-de-Boeuf, running from the dungeon to the sound of the horn.

In another room of the castle, trembling Rebecca stood on the edge of a balcony and threatened to jump.

"You shall not have me," she warned Bois Guilbert, who came toward her. "Don't come any closer!" Just then, the horn sounded.

Rowena, too, was caught. She had refused De Bracy. Then he told her about Ivanhoe and said if she did not consent to marry him, he would give Ivanhoe to Front-de-Boeuf. She knew the cruel Front-de-Boeuf wanted Ivanhoe's lands and would surely kill him for them. She broke down and cried just as the horn sounded.

Cedric and Athelstane thought of escape - when the blast of the horn sounded.

A messenger at the gate said if the prisoners were not freed, the castle would be taken by force.

"Never. Within the hour, Cedric and Athelstane shall hang by their necks in full view from the tower balcony," Front-de-Boeuf snarled.

No time to waste if the prisoners were to be saved!

The attack on the castle began immediately. Locksley's men showered the walls with arrows. When a Norman soldier dared to show himself above the walls, he was struck down.

Then Front-de-Boeuf rode out through the gate to meet the Black Knight. They threw themselves at one another with fury, sword and battle-ax.

The Black Knight was too strong and swift for Front-de-Boeuf. A broad swing of the battle-ax and Front-de-Boeuf fell from his horse and lay dying in the dirt.

Soon the castle fell. But Bois Guilbert, with Rebecca as his prisoner, plunged his horse through the attackers to escape. Athelstane, now free, challenged him. The Knight Templar struck swiftly with the broad sword and Athelstane, with a blow to the head, fell to the ground. To all he appeared dead and was carried away.

Then De Bracy, with the Black Knight's sword at his throat, surrendered and was allowed to live.

"I spare you for a reason, traitor. Go tell my brother, Prince John, I will be coming for him," said the Black Knight, removing his helmet and showing himself as King Richard to the surprised De Bracy.

Isaac, hearing Rebecca had been taken by Bois Guilbert, fell to the ground wailing, "My beautiful Rebecca. What shall I do?"

"Be of hope, Isaac," said Locksley. "Let us arrange a ransom. Those thieving Normans like nothing better than gold."

Set free by Richard, it wasn't long before De Bracy reached York and Prince John. John was in deep trouble. Richard was loose and coming for him. Without Isaac's money, he could not raise an army.

"What we can't do openly with an army we will have to do in secret to end Richard's rule," the prince said.

The job of getting rid of Richard was given to Fitzurse. With six of his best men, good with knife and sword, Fitzurse left York at twilight looking to surprise Richard.

A CASTLE FALLS

COMPREHENSION CHECK

Choose the best answer.

1. The Clerk of Copmanhurst was also known as
   ___a. Father Tuck.
   ___b. Friar Tuck.
   ___c. Friar Dunstan.
   ___d. Friar Front-de-Boeuf.

2. Besides caring for the church, Friar Tuck
   ___a. stole from the poor.
   ___b. stole from the monks.
   ___c. was one of Robin Hood's outlaws.
   ___d. was a mighty Norman conqueror.

3. The Black Knight had asked Friar Tuck for
   ___a. money.
   ___b. a hot meal.
   ___c. a place to live.
   ___d. food and shelter for one night.

4. As Friar Tuck spoke with the Black Knight, who came to the door?
   ___a. Robin Hood
   ___b. Ivanhoe
   ___c. Prince John
   ___d. Bois Guilbert

5. First, Locksley told the Black Knight about the attack and of Ivanhoe's trouble. Then the Black Knight, along with Locksley and his men, rushed to Torquilstone. Next,
   ___a. they surrounded the castle.
   ___b. they freed the prisoners.
   ___c. they freed Isaac.
   ___d. they freed Ivanhoe.

6. Why did Rebecca threaten to jump off the balcony?
   ___a. She wanted to scare Bois Guilbert.
   ___b. She thought that if she were dead, her father would pay the ransom and be freed.
   ___c. She would rather die, than give herself to Bois Guilbert.
   ___d. She didn't like being a prisoner.

7. Who was the Black Knight?
   ___a. Prior Aymer
   ___b. King Richard
   ___c. Prince John
   ___d. Wamba, the jester

8. When Prince John learned that his brother was coming for him, what did he do?
   ___a. He killed himself.
   ___b. He left England.
   ___c. He sent an army to find Richard and kill him.
   ___d. He sent six of his best men to find Richard and kill him.

9. Another name for this story could be
   ___a. "Friar Tuck's Kindness."
   ___b. "Knights of Honor."
   ___c. "Twilight Time."
   ___d. "Attack at Torquilstone."

10. This story is mainly about
    ___a. why Rebecca wanted to jump off the balcony.
    ___b. how King Richard and Locksley and his men freed the prisoners at Torquilstone.
    ___c. the wicked ways of Front-de-Boeuf.
    ___d. why Friar Tuck became an outlaw.

Check your answers with the key on page 67.

This page may be reproduced for classroom use.

A CASTLE FALLS

VOCABULARY CHECK

balcony	broad	clerk	consent	traitor	twilight

I. Sentences to Finish

Fill in the blank in each sentence with the correct key word from the box above.

1. The _____ shared secrets with the enemy.

2. The _____ highway could handle four lanes of traffic.

3. Kay lost her step and knocked a plant over the _____ .

4. Mother would not _____ to let me drive the car.

5. Our family eats dinner in the evening, just after _____ .

6. I helped the store _____ bag the groceries.

II. Word Meanings

Choose the best answer.

1. A <u>balcony</u> is found

   ____a. on a building.
   ____b. in the river.
   ____c. in a garden.

2. If something is <u>broad</u>, it is
   ____a. narrow.
   ____b. wide.
   ____c. ugly.

3. A <u>clerk</u> can be found in
   ____a. a sandwich.
   ____b. a zoo.
   ____c. a store.

4. If you <u>consent</u> to do something, you

   ____a. argue about doing it.
   ____b. agree to do it.
   ____c. avoid doing it.

5. A <u>traitor</u> is one who
   ____a. is loyal to his country.
   ____b. betrays his country.
   ____c. defends his country.

6. <u>Twilight</u> is
   ____a. a kind of cupcake.
   ____b. found on the front of a car.
   ____c. a time of day.

Check your answers with the key on page 70.

This page may be reproduced for classroom use.

A Witch Trial for Rebecca

PREPARATION

Key Words

cell   (sel)   a small, narrow room in a prison
The prisoner was kept in a <u>cell</u> for six hours.

consider   (kən sid´ ər)   to think about carefully and seriously
A high school student should <u>consider</u> going on to college.

plead   (plēd)   to argue for or against something; to beg
He used to <u>plead</u> for extra time to stay up at night.

presence   (prez´ ns)   in the sight or company of; appearance
The children's <u>presence</u> was required in the classroom at eight o'clock in the morning.

sob   (sob)   to cry or sigh with short quick breaths
The baby would <u>sob</u> until she got her bottle.

trial   (trī´ əl)   examining and deciding a case in court
The burglar will soon be brought to <u>trial</u>.

A Witch Trial for Rebecca

Necessary Words

combat   (kom´ bat)   a fight; struggle; battle
The soldiers in <u>combat</u> showed themselves to be men of courage.

guilty   (gil´ tē)   having done wrong; deserving to be punished
The man was found to be <u>guilty</u> the crime.

kidnapped   (kid´ nappəd)   stole; to have taken by force
Someone <u>kidnapped</u> the little boy next door, but he was found and returned to his mother.

A Witch Trial for Rebecca

In the castle, Bois Guilbert locks Rebecca up in a cell.

Preview: 1. Read the name of the story.
2. Look at the picture.
3. Read the sentence under the picture.
4. Read the first paragraph of the story.
5. Then answer the following question.

You learned from your preview that when Bois Guilbert and Rebecca reached Templestowe it was
___ a. snowing.
___ b. raining.
___ c. a hot afternoon.
___ d. early in the morning.

Turn to the Comprehension Check on page 46 for the right answer.

Now read the story.

Read to find out what the Grand Master has planned for Rebecca.

A Witch Trial for Rebecca

It was dark and stormy when Bois Guilbert and Rebecca found Templestowe, the castle of the Knights Templar. Wrapped in a great cloak against the rain, Rebecca passed through the gate without being seen. Bois Guilbert soon found a cell for her in a far part of the castle and locked her in.

He told only one person about Rebecca: his friend Albert Malvoisin, the captain of the castle.

"You're mad," cried Malvoisin. "Did you not consider that the Grand Master is with us?"

The Grand Master of all Knights Templar, in England and in France, was Lucas Beaumanoir. He had been Grand Master for many years. He had no love or respect for Jews and others who were not Normans and Christians.

"If he finds you are keeping this Jew in our presence, he will strip you of your honors and deal terribly with her," warned Malvoisin.

"Then he won't find out, good friend, will he?" said Bois Guilbert. "Besides, he would never thing to come to this sorry-looking part of the castle."

"Let's pray not. Otherwise it will mean my neck as well as yours," said Malvoisin.

Now, after leaving Sherwood Forest for Templestowe to ransom Rebecca, Isaac reached a small village near the castle. There he rested for the night with an old friend, Nathan Ben Israel. He told his friend what had happened and what he intended to do.

"Isaac, you can't go to Templestowe just now. The Grand Master is visiting. He hates our people."

"I'll plead. I'll make him an offer he can't refuse. If he'll just give me back my dear Rebecca."

Next morning, Isaac stood before the main gate at Templestowe and asked to see the Grand Master.

"This dog of a merchant asks for me?" snarled the Grand Master. "I'll have his head! Bring him here."

Poor Isaac, trembling, was brought before the Grand Master.

"Speak. And if the words aren't right, I'll have you beaten and thrown into a dungeon."

"Oh, mighty lord. Never would I come if the best part of me were not already here within these walls."

"What? What's this nonsense you speak?"

"Mighty lord. My daughter Rebecca. She was brought here by Brian de Bois Guilbert as a prisoner. I'll pay any ransom you ask - all I have - for her release," Isaac pleaded.

"Good God!" roared the Grand Master. "Your daughter within *these* walls? With our champion Bois Guilbert? Bring me the captain, and throw this dog out of the castle!"

"But my Rebecca," cried Isaac, with a loud sob.

"Out! Out! Take him out of my presence!" roared the Grand Master.

Sobbing and pleading, Isaac was dragged from the hall. He was beaten by the guards and left in the road outside the gate.

Nathan Ben Israel who had come with his friend as far as the castle, helped him to his feet. "Come back with me to the house, my friend. We'll think of something," he said.

Albert Malvoisin studied the Grand Master as he entered the hall. He knew of only one thing that could make him this angry.

"Explain why you allowed Bois Guilbert to bring this Jew into the castle," the Grand Master demanded.

"My lord," said Malvoisin, thinking quickly, "it was to protect him. Rebecca seems to have cast a spell on him. I thought if I could separate them in the castle, I could bring our champion to his senses," he lied.

"Ah, a spell. I knew it!" stormed the Grand Master. "I am told she was taught the healing arts by that Miriam, who was burned as a witch."

"Indeed she was taught by Miriam," Malvoisin said.

"Then she too must be a witch, and we shall bring her to trial. Make the arrangements."

Bois Guilbert could not believe his ears. He kidnapped Rebecca and now the poor girl was to be tried as a witch. She would be found guilty and would be burned at the stake.

"Malvoisin. The girl is innocent. You must help me get her away from here," cried Bois Guilbert.

"Consider your future. You will lose everything if you leave with her. But if she is found by trial to be a witch, the Grand Master will forgive you. He will think you were in her power," said Malvoisin.

Later, Bois Guilbert visited Rebecca's cell and told her about the trial.

"God will protect me," Rebecca said.

"If you will leave the castle with me and be my own forever, God will *surely* protect you," said Bois Guilbert.

"Never," said Rebecca. "I'll stand trial."

Bois Guilbert stormed out of the room.

The trial took place the next morning. All the Knights Templar were there and many of the common people. Rebecca was soon found guilty of witchcraft, but before the Grand Master could pass sentence, she spoke out.

"I believe I may demand a trial-by-combat," she said. "And I may choose a knight to prove my innocence against the court's knight."

"That is so," the Grand Master said. "Your knight will meet our knight, Bois Guilbert, here in three days."

Bois Guilbert went white when he heard he would be the court's knight. With Ivanhoe badly wounded, there was not a knight in all of England who had a chance of defeating him and saving this poor girl. She will die and it is my fault, he thought, now hating himself.

A Witch Trial for Rebecca

COMPREHENSION CHECK

Choose the best answer.

1. Templestowe
   ___a. was Bois Guilbert's best friend.
   ___b. was a Knight Templar.
   ___c. was captain of the Knights Templar.
   ___d. was the castle of the Knights Templar.

2. Bois Guilbert told only one person that he was hiding Rebecca in the castle. Who was it?
   ___a. Malvoisin
   ___b. Lucas Beaumanoir
   ___c. The Grand Master
   ___d. Nathan Ben Israel

3. Lucas Beaumanoir, Grand Master of the Knights Templar, was
   ___a. a kind person.
   ___b. a cruel man.
   ___c. a man everyone had respect for.
   ___d. the King of France.

4. When Isaac told the Grand Master that his daughter was within the walls of the castle, why did the Grand Master get angry?
   ___a. He didn't invite Rebecca to the castle.
   ___b. Bois Guilbert did not ask if he could bring her there.
   ___c. He was upset that a Jew was in the castle.
   ___d. He didn't like young women.

5. Because Isaac loved his daughter, he was willing to
   ___a. plead for his daughter's life.
   ___b. make himself look foolish in front of the Grand Master.
   ___c. place his own life in danger.
   ___d. give the Grand Master some of his riches.

6. Malvoisin told the Grand Master that Rebecca cast a spell on Bois Guilbert. Why did he lie?
   ___a. To get Rebecca into trouble
   ___b. To save the necks of Bois Guilbert and himself
   ___c. To bring the Grand Master to his senses
   ___d. He thought his lie would help the young girl

7. When Bois Guilbert learned that Rebecca was to stand trial for witchcraft,
   ___a. he pleaded with Malvoisin to help him sneak Rebecca out of the castle.
   ___b. he pleaded with the Grand Master to let her go.
   ___c. he went looking for Ivanhoe.
   ___d. he asked Rebecca to forgive him.

8. Just as the Grand Master was about to sentence Rebecca, she spoke out and demanded
   ___a. to see her father.
   ___b. to see Ivanhoe.
   ___c. a fair trial.
   ___d. a trial-by-combat.

9. Another name for this story could be
   ___a. "Spoken Like a True Witch!"
   ___b. "Malvoisin's Lie."
   ___c. "Rebecca's Secret."
   ___d. "A Night at Templestowe."

10. This story is mainly about
    ___a. Isaac's love for his daughter.
    ___b. Bois Guilbert's love for Rebecca.
    ___c. how Rebecca had come to be locked up in the castle.
    ___d. how a young girl had come to stand trial for witchcraft.

Check your answers with the key on page 67.

This page may be reproduced for classroom use.

A Witch Trial for Rebecca

VOCABULARY CHECK

cell	consider	plead	presence	sob	trial

I. Sentences to Finish

Fill in the blank in each sentence with the correct key word from the box above.

1. The thief was put in a _____ until it was time to go to court.

2. At his _____ , the accused man was asked to tell his story.

3. When the soldier was caught, he was brought in the _____ of his enemies.

4. I heard the baby _____ when she dropped her bottle.

5. I will _____ with my father to lend me his car on Saturday.

6. When Bob asked me for a date, I said I would _____ it.

II. Matching

Write the letter of the correct meaning from Column B next to the key word in Column A.

Column A

____1. cell

____2. sob

____3. trial

____4. plead

____5. consider

____6. presence

Column B

a. examining and deciding a case in court

b. to think about carefully and seriously

c. a small, narrow room in a prison

d. to cry or sigh with short, quick breaths

e. in the sight or company of; appearance

f. to argue for or against something; to beg

Check your answers with the key on page 71.

This page may be reproduced for classroom use.

To Burn at the Stake

PREPARATION

Key Words

concern	(kən-súrn´)	regard for or interest in someone or something; worry *The doctor's <u>concern</u> for the patient helped to speed her healing.*
failure	(fāl´ yər)	not achieving the desired end *My attempt to climb to the top of the mountain ended in <u>failure</u>.*
glory	(glô´ rē)	great honor; praise *<u>Glory</u> comes to the general whose army wins the battle.*
justice	(jus´ tis)	that which is right and fair; making sure what is right and fair happens or is protected *<u>Justice</u> is getting kept after school for not doing your homework.*
oppose	(ə-pōz´)	to be against or to resist *I voted to <u>oppose</u> the closing of the library.*
volunteer	(vol´ən-tir´)	a person who performs any service of his own free will *Jim was happy to <u>volunteer</u> to help his neighbor paint his house.*

To Burn at the Stake

Necessary Words

crossroad   (krôs´ rōd´)   a place where two or more roads meet
Turn left at the <u>crossroad</u> to get to my house.

Places

Jerusalem   is the capital of Israel.

Priory of Saint Botolph   is a religious community of monks in England.

Spain   is a country in Europe.

To Burn at the Stake

Rebecca pleads for someone to take a message to her father.

Preview: 1. Read the name of the story.
           2. Look at the picture.
           3. Read the sentence under the picture.
           4. Read the first four paragraphs of the story.
           5. Then answer the following question.

You learned from your preview that Rebecca was looking for a volunteer
who would
___ a. sneak her out of the castle.
___ b. kill the Grand Master.
___ c. marry her.
___ d. take a message to Isaac in York.

Turn to the Comprehension Check on page 52 for the right answer.

Now read the story.

Read to find out how Bois Guilbert feels about what he has done.

To Burn at the Stake

Word reached Nathan Ben Israel that a witchcraft trial was being held at the castle. He and Isaac, with great concern showing, hurried there and waited at the crossroad beyond the walls.

Inside, before the Grand Master, stood Rebecca, pleading. "Who will take my message?" she cried out, looking around the hall of cold faces.

None would volunteer. She had just three days to find a knight - a champion of her innocence. Certainly none of these knights would fight for her. She must get a message to Isaac in York.

"Where is your justice?" she cried out the louder. "I'm allowed a knight and it must be arranged!"

Then Higg, a carpenter, came forward. "I will take your message, mistress."

Higg had been a witness to Rebecca's healing powers. He told the court that Rebecca had healed him when he fell sick while working for Isaac. She had given him secret medicines, and he had healed. Secret medicines? Why, that's witchcraft, decided the court. (These were foolish times.) So Higg, by telling how he was made well, only made it worse for Rebecca. As a witness, Higg was a failure.

"Here, good Higg, take this note to my father, Isaac, in York. He will reward you for your service."

Higg rushed from the hall and went out of the castle. He found his mule and rode it to the crossroad where, to his great surprise, he found Isaac and Nathan.

"Isaac," spoke Higg, "I was prepared to carry a message to you in York from Rebecca."

Isaac took the note from Higg and began to read. His face reddened, his hands shook, and his body rocked back and forth.

"They say my Rebecca is a witch. They want to burn her at the stake. Her only escape is a trial-by-combat." Isaac read on. "Merciful God! Her champion must fight that evil Bois Guilbert who carried her off. There isn't a knight in all of England or France who can defeat him - except Ivanhoe, who is wounded and too weak to lift his sword. Yet Rebecca sees the wounded knight as her only hope. 'Go to him,' she pleads. 'He will decide what is to be done for me.'"

Isaac knew only that Ivanhoe had been freed when Torquilstone had fallen to Locksley and his men and the Black Knight. He could not have known that the Black Knight took charge of Ivanhoe and freed him from the castle. Nor did he know that the Black Knight was King Richard, and Ivanhoe, his most trusted knight who fought side-by-side and back-to-back with him in the Holy Land wars.

"My lord. Let me ride with you now," Ivanhoe had said, when he was freed.

"Time enough, young Wilfred of Ivanhoe. I will need you fully healed and strong if my brother, Prince John, and his friends truly intend to oppose me."

That said, the Black Knight arranged to have Ivanhoe delivered on his cot to the Priory of Saint Botolph. There he became the concern of the prior, himself a famous healer.

How would Isaac ever find Ivanhoe? He hadn't a clue where to look. Would there be time to save Rebecca?

Inside the castle, Bois Guilbert stopped speaking. His face would go white, then turn red, then blacken. His eyes were like two black stones. His lips pressed tightly against his teeth. His fellow knights stared and saw a war going on inside him. They stayed clear of him.

After the trial, Bois Guilbert again visited Rebecca in her cell.

"All is lost, girl. No one will volunteer to oppose me because no one can defeat me. You will be set on fire and die slowly and horribly, unless you accept me. Come away with me. We will go to Spain, or to Jerusalem. I will raise an army and be a king. You will be my queen and have more glory than you ever dreamed of."

"No," said Rebecca. "I am what I am and you are what you are. We can never be together. I will accept God's justice in the trial-by-combat, whatever happens."

Then Bois Guilbert's appearance began to change. Out of him, like air escaping a balloon, went all hope of success. Rushing in, came a sense of failure and rage. The proud knight lost all hope of having Rebecca and all interest in the glory and riches of the world. Every part of him now felt blame for what was happening to Rebecca. And, like boiling water, the rage spilled over him because he could do nothing to save her. How he hated himself for what he had done!

To Burn at the Stake

COMPREHENSION CHECK

Choose the best answer.

Preview Answer:
d. take a message to Isaac in York.

1. Who finally came forward to take Rebecca's message to her father?
   ___a. Nathan Ben Israel
   ___b. Bois Guilbert
   ___c. Higg
   ___d. Isaac

2. Higg only made it worse for Rebecca by telling the court that
   ___a. Rebecca was his mistress.
   ___b. he would take Rebecca's message to Isaac.
   ___c. Rebecca was a witch.
   ___d. Rebecca had healed him.

3. Higg
   ___a. did not mean to cause more trouble for Rebecca.
   ___b. was a good witness.
   ___c. was a foolish man.
   ___d. was nothing but a failure.

4. Higg found Isaac and Nathan
   ___a. in York.
   ___b. at the crossroad.
   ___c. at the castle gate.
   ___d. at Torquilstone.

5. In her message, Rebecca pleaded with her father to
   ___a. free her.
   ___b. pay a ransom to set her free.
   ___c. find the Black Knight.
   ___d. find Ivanhoe.

6. Isaac
   ___a. did not know where to find Ivanhoe.
   ___b. rode to the Priory of Saint Botolph to get Ivanhoe.
   ___c. headed back to Torquilstone where he last saw Ivanhoe.
   ___d. gave up all hope of helping his daughter.

7. What was happening to Rebecca made Bois Guilbert feel
   ___a. lucky.
   ___b. proud.
   ___c. that he was to blame.
   ___d. successful.

8. Rebecca's decision to let the trial-by-combat continue, no matter what happened, showed Rebecca to be
   ___a. a stubborn woman.
   ___b. a foolish woman.
   ___c. a brave woman.
   ___d. a crazy woman.

9. Another name for this story could be
   ___a. "Rebecca Stands Firm."
   ___b. "Bois Guilbert's Promise."
   ___c. "The Foolish Carpenter."
   ___d. "Justice at the Castle."

10. This story is mainly about
    ___a. Isaac's search for Ivanhoe.
    ___b. Bois Guilbert's rage.
    ___c. a brave young woman's fight to save herself.
    ___d. a young woman who refused to get married.

Check your answers with the key on page 67.

To Burn at the Stake

VOCABULARY CHECK

concern	failure	glory	justice	oppose	volunteer

I. Sentences to Finish

Fill in the blank in each sentence with the correct key word from the box above.

1. I will _____ to help Mother with the dishes.

2. Our picnic was a _____ because it rained all day.

3. The thief felt he received no _____ during his trial.

4. Dad will _____ the town's decision to build another road.

5. Parents show great _____ for the safety of their children.

6. The swift victory brought _____ to the team.

II. Use the blank spaces to write the words that do not belong.

1. Which word does <u>not</u> belong with concern?
    a. interest   b. duty   c. worry   _____

2. Which word does <u>not</u> belong with failure?
    a. support   b. loss   c. defeat   _____

3. Which word does <u>not</u> belong with glory?
    a. priase   b. honor   c. pity   _____

4. Which word does <u>not</u> belong with justice?
    a. final   b. fairness   c. right   _____

5. Which word does <u>not</u> belong with oppose?
    a. resist   b. fight   c. obey   _____

6. Which word does <u>not</u> belong with volunteer?
    a. coax   b. give   c. offer   _____

Check your answers with the key on page 71.

Farewell to Athelstane

PREPARATION

Key Words

accompany	(ə-kum´pə nē)	to go along with *Lisa will <u>accompany</u> us to dinner.*
elm	(elm)	a certain type of tree that sheds its leaves and has curving branches *We sat in the shade of the large <u>elm</u> tree.*
occasion	(ə kā´ zhən)	1. an event or happening; a favorable time *A wedding is a happy <u>occasion</u>.* 2. from time to time; now and then *<u>On occasion</u>, we go out for dinner.*
pierce	(pirs)	1. to cut or pass through *The alarm would <u>pierce</u> the noise in the gym.* 2. stab *If your car runs over a nail it might <u>pierce</u> a tire.*
seek	(sēk)	to try to locate or discover something; search for *When you're "it" in Hide-And-Go-Seek, you <u>seek</u> the others in their hiding places.*
solid	(sol´id)	hearty; without gaps or breaks; well made *A <u>solid</u> sheet of ice caused the cars to slip all over the highway.*

Farewell to Athelstane

Necessary Words

clanking   (klangk´ ing)   making the sound like the rattle of a heavy metal chain

> *You could hear the <u>clanking</u> of swords as the battle began.*

confession   (kən fesh´ ən)   the act of admitting something

> *It was the thief's <u>confession</u> that landed him in prison.*

description   (di skrip´ shən)   a telling in words of how a person, place, thing or event looks like or behaves

> *I gave the policeman a <u>description</u> of the robber.*

Things

chain-mail   armor made of joined metal links

Farewell to Athelstane

*The two knights and Wamba prepare to leave
for Coningsburgh to attend Athelstane's funeral.*

Preview:
1. Read the name of the story.
2. Look at the picture.
3. Read the sentence under the picture.
4. Read the first five paragraphs of the story.
5. Then answer the following question.

You learned from your preview that Ivanhoe
___ a. had gotten well.
___ b. was too badly wounded to travel.
___ c. was dying.
___ d. had pretended to be wounded all along.

Turn to the Comprehension Check on page 58 for the right answer.

Now read the story.

Read to find out what happens to the Black Knight and Ivanhoe on their
way to Coningsburgh.

Farewell to Athelstane

Soon enough, the Black Knight joined Ivanhoe at the Priory of Saint Botolph. Almost overnight, he had gotten well.

"Hah! Good Saxon food and fresh milk from a fat Saxon cow agrees with you, young man. You look fit to ride, if not to fight."

"That I am, lord. And I see we have a jester with us to make the occasion merry," said Ivanhoe.

Wamba, knowing the Black Knight was King Richard and riding alone, chose to accompany him as squire. He carried the long hunting horn Locksley had given the Black Knight on the day they parted. "If you ever need me in these woods, give two solid blasts of the horn and, before you can say Prince John, my men will be surrounding you," Locksley had promised.

"We leave for Coningsburgh, the castle of the fallen Athelstane, to attend his funeral," said the Black Knight. "Cedric will be in charge of the farewell to his Saxon lord and friend. I seek to bring you and Cedric together again, young Wilfred. And I seek to make a friend of Cedric. Saxon and Norman must be brothers in the new England I see."

The two knights and jester rode off toward Coningsburgh. After an hour, they were deep in the woods of Sherwood Forest, ducking the low, solid limbs of a stand of old elm trees and moving slowly. Suddenly, they were attacked. Hands reached for Wamba and threw him to the ground. From behind, Ivanhoe was struck on the head with a quarter-staff, and fell to the ground, unmoving.

The Black Knight freed his sword and was slashing with it. Two of his attackers felt its deadly cut. A third attacker backed away. Then the loud blast of a hunting horn sounded. And then a second blast. Wamba had gotten free and sounded the alarm. Shouts in the forest could now be heard.

At that moment, a knight in blue armor rode out of the trees with sword drawn to attack the Black Knight from behind. The Black Knight was unaware of the danger. A straight-ahead thrust of the broad sword would surely pierce the chain-mail armor across the Black Knight's broad back. A killing thrust it would be.

Wamba was nearest and saw it all. He jumped the Blue Knight's horse as it passed and cut the saddle strap cleanly with his knife. Knight and saddle slipped from the horse's back and fell to the ground with a loud, clanking sound. Before the knight could get to his feet, he was surrounded by Locksley's men springing out of the woods.

"Let me see this fellow," the Black Knight said, making his way to the Blue Knight who still lay tangled in his saddle. Lifting his helmet, he was surprised to see that it was Fitzurse.

"Traitor. You deserve death, but I will spare you. Go back and tell Prince John that King Richard is coming for him. Then leave England. I spare your life for just three days."

More than a blow from a quarter-staff was needed to keep Ivanhoe down for long. The young knight, still weakened from his wounds, was helped to his feet.

Then Locksley and his men were treated to a surprise. The Black Knight removed his helmet and spoke.

"Your king thanks you, Locksley. You and your men will have your reward when I, Richard, King of England, claim my throne."

For a long moment the only sound in the forest was the wind piercing the leafy elm trees. Then came an explosion of men's voices. "Long live King Richard, long live King Richard, long live King Richard."

Locksley, bowing to his king, approached. "My lord, I have a confession. Locksley is a name I use on occasion. You may have heard worse of me as Robin Hood. These men before you, and I, are outlaws."

King Richard did not seem surprised. "I suspected you were he. But with good reason you became outlaws - when there was no justice for Saxons!

Now you are my loyal subjects, and you have my promise that there will be justice in England for Norman and Saxon."

Poor Isaac would have given his fortune to have been given that promise for his people and himself. In this cruel land, only his money could protect Rebecca and himself, he thought. But now he wasn't even sure of that. In Isaac's name, large sums of money were offered to past champion-knights to fight Bois Guilbert. None would challenge the Knight Templar, even for great wealth.

"Where, oh, where is Ivanhoe?" he said aloud. He had sent out his servants to the main roads leading to the towns and the castles. All but one returned. No one had seen or heard about Ivanhoe, or anyone fitting his description. The trial-by-combat was set for the following day.

Then hope reappeared as the last servant returned. "I saw him, Master Isaac, traveling slowly, accompanied by a large knight in black armor. They were on the road that leads to Coningsburgh, the castle of the Saxon lord, Athelstane."

"Of course," said Isaac. "They said Athelstane was killed at Torquilstone. They are attending his funeral. My best and swiftest horse! Hurry!"

Farewell to Athelstane

COMPREHENSION CHECK

Choose the best answer.

Preview Answer:
a. had gotten well.

1. King Richard, Ivanhoe, and Wamba headed for Coningsburgh to
   ___a. attend a tournament.
   ___b. attend a party for Athelstane.
   ___c. attend Athelstane's funeral.
   ___d. find Cedric.

2. After an hour, the two knights and jester were
   ___a. too tired to go on.
   ___b. lost.
   ___c. attacked.
   ___d. hungry.

3. As they fought off their attackers, Wamba broke free and
   ___a. blew his hunting horn.
   ___b. ran for help.
   ___c. ran away.
   ___d. hid behind a tree.

4. Wamba watched as the Blue Knight prepared to attack King Richard from behind. Next, Wamba jumped the knight's horse and cut the saddle strap, knocking knight and horse to the ground. Then,
   ___a. King Richard removed the Blue Knight's helmet.
   ___b. King Richard spared the Blue Knight's life.
   ___c. King Richard ordered the Blue Knight to leave England.
   ___d. Locksley's men sprang out of the woods.

5. Wamba
   ___a. had caused much trouble.
   ___b. had saved the king's life.
   ___c. had saved Ivanhoe.
   ___d. had never used his knife before.

6. When the Black Knight removed his helmet, showing himself to be the king, Locksley and his men were
   ___a. pleasantly surprised.
   ___b. very disappointed.
   ___c. awfully confused.
   ___d. frozen with fear.

7. Locksley confessed to the king that he and his men
   ___a. had been loyal to Prince John.
   ___b. were good citizens.
   ___c. were dangerous men.
   ___d. were outlaws.

8. King Richard promised that
   ___a. his brother would pay dearly for his bad deeds.
   ___b. there would be justice for all the people of England.
   ___c. Locksley would be the heir to his throne.
   ___d. all Normans would be forced to leave England.

9. Another name for this story could be
   ___a. "Richard's Throne."
   ___b. "Richard Spares a Life."
   ___c. "The King's Promise for a New England."
   ___d. "Isaac Continues his Search."

10. This story is mainly about
    ___a. how Prince John's plan to kill his brother, failed.
    ___b. Isaac and his mad search for Ivanhoe.
    ___c. the courage of a court jester.
    ___d. King Richard's promise to reward Locksley and his men.

Check your answers with the key on page 67.

Farewell to Athelstane

VOCABULARY CHECK

| accompany | elm | occasion | pierce | seek | solid |

I. Sentences to Finish

Fill in the blank in each sentence with the correct key word from the box above.

1. My mother will _____ our class on our trip to the museum.

2. The teacher asked me to _____ information about the Bermuda Triangle.

3. On _____ , Dad will let me use his car.

4. When the sun gets hot, we seek shade under the _____ tree.

5. The candy bunny is made of _____ chocolate.

6. Andy aimed his arrow and hoped to _____ his target.

II. Word Use

Put a check next to YES if the sentence makes sense. Put a check next to NO if the sentence does not make sense.

1. The door was easy to break down; it was made of <u>solid</u> steel. _____ YES _____ NO

2. If you <u>pierce</u> a balloon with a pin, it will burst. _____ YES _____ NO

3. Sarah's birthday party was a happy <u>occasion</u> for all who came. _____ YES _____ NO

4. Ted will stay home and <u>accompany</u> his brother to the show. _____ YES _____ NO

5. The <u>elm</u> tree in our backyard gives us plenty of shade. _____ YES _____ NO

6. Ida's mother told her to <u>seek</u> new homes for the little kittens. _____ YES _____ NO

Check your answers with the key on page 71.

A Champion Once Again

PREPARATION

Key Words

cape	(kāp)	a sleeveless garment fastened at the throat and worn hanging over the shoulders *It was such a cool day, Jane decided to wear her new cape.*
drain	(drān)	empty out *We all watched the hungry baby drain his bottle.*
lurch	(lėrch)	to stagger *The horse appeared to lurch forward when the starting gun was fired.*
monk	(mungk)	a churchman who lives, works and prays with others of his kind *The young monk was praying in the church.*
pardon	(pärd´n)	forgive *"Pardon me for stepping on your toes."*
torch	(tôrch)	a light made by wrapping material around the end of a stick of wood and setting it on fire *The man carried a torch as he made his way through the dark tunnel.*

A Champion Once Again

Necessary Words

baron (bar´ ən) a lord or nobleman
The wise <u>baron</u> was loved by all.

coffin (kô´ fən) a long box in which a dead body is put to be buried
He must have been very rich, for his <u>coffin</u> was made of gold.

heir (ãr) a person who has the right to someone's property after that person dies
Samuel is the only <u>heir</u> to his father's riches.

inheritance (in her´ i təns) money or property that is received from another person after that person's death; something left to an heir
Joe received a large <u>inheritance</u> from his Uncle Michael.

A Champion Once Again

Athelstane's body is carried to the castle for his funeral.

Preview: 1. Read the name of the story.
2. Look at the picture.
3. Read the sentence under the picture.
4. Read the first two paragraphs of the story.
5. Then answer the following question.

You learned from your preview that Athelstane
___ a. had cared for the monks.
___ b. had been cruel to the monks.
___ c. had put all the monks in prison.
___ d. had given loyal service to the monks.

Turn to the Comprehension Check on page 64 for the right answer.

Now read the story.

Read to find out what happens at Coningsburgh.

A Champion Once Again

The Saxons came to Coningsburgh for Athelstane's funeral. His body was taken from Torquilstone, where he was struck down, to St. Edmund's, a church nearby. Then monks from St. Edmund's carried him to the castle for the funeral. Or so all thought.

For years, Athelstane's family had cared for the monks, paying money into their purses. The monks were even counted among Athelstane's heirs. They would get even larger sums upon his death. In return, the monks gave loyal service to the family.

The Black Knight and Ivanhoe came to Coningsburgh. Ivanhoe hid his face in the folds of a great cape. Soon they were alone in a private room with Cedric.

"Good Cedric," the Black Knight began, "I would collect the favor you pledged when you and your friends were freed."

"Name it, Sir Knight," said Cedric.

He removed his helmet. "Before you stands Richard, King of England. And with him, your son, Wilfred."

Cedric was startled. He looked on Wilfred, his face now out of the cape. He could not reply.

"Evil men would steal my throne and keep Norman and Saxon enemies. I need your support. Norman and Saxon must be treated as equals . . . and fathers and sons must be together. I call on you to pardon Wilfred."

That was just what stubborn Cedric needed to hear - a shove that made him do what he secretly wanted to do. He seemed to lurch toward Wilfred. He held him tightly.

Then from below came loud shouts. Then loud steps on the stairs to the room. Lurching through the door came Athelstane . . . or his ghost!

"Oh, God," groaned Cedric, as the blood from his face seemed to drain.

"But I saw the man struck down!" roared Richard.

"God keep us!" shouted Ivanhoe.

"Will no one offer me a drink or some food? I'm starved," wailed Athelstane.

"Is it really you?" asked Cedric.

"Food and drink and I'll tell you all."

He drained the cup and began his story.

"Indeed I caught the Knight Templar's blade on the head," he said, "but it was the flat of the sword. It glanced off my sword. I was without helmet and went down.

"Lying among the bodies at the end of the battle, I was mistaken for dead. I was carried to St. Edmund's, where the monks took charge. Some time later I awoke to find myself lying in a coffin. Monks praying by the side of the coffin were startled by my moans. They whispered, then gave me wine. It contained something that put me into a deep sleep.

"When I awoke, the lid was on the coffin. Why, they planned to bury me - dead or alive - and collect the inheritance! But I was strong. I forced the lid off, climbed out, filled the coffin with heavy stones, and put the lid back on. Then I escaped, and here I am; starved and tired - and very angry. They'll hang; every last one of them," he finished.

As he was telling his story, Rowena entered.

"Dear Lady. Your pardon, but it's time for us to face the truth. Never again will there be a Saxon kingdom. There's no reason for you and I to marry. You and Wilfred belong together. I'm ready to call Richard my king."

All turned looking for Ivanhoe, but he was no longer in the room.

"I brought him a message from Isaac of York, who came into the courtyard. They talked and then rode off," a servant said.

At Templestowe, Rebecca was brought onto the field of battle. She was lifted to a chair on top of a large pile of firewood. The chair leaned against a thick, wooden stake in the pile. She was tied to the chair and the stake.

Knights Templar and common people filled the viewing stands. Bois Guilbert waited to face Rebecca's champion. All morning he waited.

The Grand Master spoke. "We will wait until the light begins to fail. If no one comes to defend her, put a torch to the wood."

Through the afternoon, Rebecca prayed quietly. Helmet off, Bois Guilbert's face was a mask of pain. He muttered to himself and ground his teeth. Then a servant carrying a torch walked toward Rebecca and the wood.

Then came shouting. "He comes. He comes!"

Ivanhoe rode onto the field and stopped before the Grand Master.

"I am the lady's champion."

"Then let the trial-by-combat begin," replied the Grand Master.

On snorting horses, they waited the signal. Then the two knights - deadly enemies - flew at one another. Lances found targets at the same instant; Bois Guilbert's to the helmet; Ivanhoe's to the shield. Both knights fell heavily to the ground. Ivanhoe got to his knees, but Bois Guilbert lay still and squires came to him. They bent over him, removed his helmet, then rose.

"The Knight Templar is dead, but there is no wound."

No one could explain how Bois Guilbert died that day; it was as though the life in him found his body an unwelcome place and simply left.

Rebecca was freed. She thought often of Ivanhoe, but he belonged to another. She and Isaac left England for Spain.

As expected, Ivanhoe married Rowena.

Big-hearted King Richard pardoned evil Prince John. A few years later, King Richard died and John became king. He was as bad as ever. The barons threatened to rise up against his rule. John was forced to give them a bill of rights, which was called the Magna Carta.

𝔄 Champion Once Again

COMPREHENSION CHECK

Choose the best answer.

1. What was the favor King Richard asked of Cedric?
   ___a. To support his effort to reclaim his throne
   ___b. To forgive his Norman brothers
   ___c. To help him destroy his enemies in England
   ___d. To pardon his son, Wilfred of Ivanhoe

2. Cedric
   ___a. was eager to forgive his son.
   ___b. did not trust his son.
   ___c. did not have the power to pardon anyone.
   ___d. would never forgive young Wilfred of Ivanhoe.

3. Everyone was shocked to learn that
   ___a. King Richard had returned to England.
   ___b. Cedric had pardoned his son.
   ___c. Athelstane was alive and well.
   ___d. Athelstane had grown very old.

4. According to Athelstane's story, when the monks learned that Athelstane was still alive,
   ___a. they called a doctor immediately.
   ___b. they became drunk with wine.
   ___c. they planned a celebration.
   ___d. they planned to bury him anyway.

5. In the end, Athelstane, once again, pledged loyalty to King Richard. What do you suppose changed his mind?
   ___a. His deep love for Rowena
   ___b. His close brush with death gave him a chance to rethink his life.
   ___c. He didn't want to be known as a traitor.
   ___d. He didn't want King Richard for an enemy.

6. When a servant delivered Isaac's message to Ivanhoe,
   ___a. he sobbed.
   ___b. he flew into a rage.
   ___c. he left for Templestowe to rescue Rebecca.
   ___d. he got sick to his stomach.

7. At Templestowe, Bois Guilbert
   ___a. waited to face Rebecca's champion.
   ___b. pleaded with the Grand Master to let Rebecca go.
   ___c. waited for the sun to go down.
   ___d. waited for the news that Rebecca was dead.

8. In the end, what killed Bois Guilbert?
   ___a. A deep wound in his side
   ___b. A severe blow to his head
   ___c. His horse
   ___d. No one could ever explain how he died.

9. Another name for this story could be
   ___a. "Ivanhoe Gets Married."
   ___b. "Buried Alive."
   ___c. "Rebecca's Prayers are Answered."
   ___d. "Ghosts."

10. This story is mainly about
   ___a. a king who was determined to reclaim his throne and bring justice to all his subjects in England.
   ___b. how Bois Guilbert's love for Rebecca killed him.
   ___c. how Athelstane came back to life.
   ___d. Ivanhoe's respect for King Richard.

Check your answers with the key on page 67.

This page may be reproduced for classroom use.

A Champion Once Again

VOCABULARY CHECK

cape	drain	lurch	monk	pardon	torch

I. Sentences to Finish

Fill in the blank in each sentence with the correct key word from the box above.

1. The nurse wore a _____ over her uniform.

2. "Please _____ me, but I forgot your name."

3. The man carried a _____ into the dark cave to help him find his way.

4. At the end of the summer, Dad will _____ the water from the pool.

5. The wounded man seemed to _____ forward.

6. The _____ wore a long robe tied at the waist with a cord.

II. Put an X next to the sentence in which the underlined key word is used correctly.

1. ____a. Jim ate a <u>monk</u> every morning for breakfast.
   ____b. The <u>monk</u> said a prayer for the sick child.

2. ____a. "<u>Pardon</u> me for helping you with your work."
   ____b. "<u>Pardon</u> me for hitting your parked car."

3. ____a. The strong winds caused the ship to <u>lurch</u> among the waves.
   ____b. Jim asked the <u>lurch</u> to stop following him to school.

4. ____a. He lit the <u>torch</u> to find his way in the tunnel.
   ____b. John ate a <u>torch</u> every day for lunch.

5. ____a. Tom will <u>drain</u> the fish tank and add new water.
   ____b. Ned helped the farmer <u>drain</u> his cow.

6. ____a. Jennifer wore a beautiful <u>cape</u> in her hair.
   ____b. Laura wore a beautiful <u>cape</u> that matched her red dress.

Check your answers with the key on page 72.

NOTES

COMPREHENSION CHECK ANSWER KEY
Lessons CTR E-51 to CTR E-60

LESSON NUMBER	QUESTION NUMBER										PAGE NUMBER
	1	2	3	4	5	6	7	8	9	10	
CTR E-51	d	c	a	◇b	○c	a	c	b	△a	□a	10
CTR E-52	b	○a	d	c	b	c	a	b	△d	□a	16
CTR E-53	c	○a	c	◇d	○c	b	○a	c	△b	□d	22
CTR E-54	c	a	d	b	d	a	c	○c	△a	□d	28
CTR E-55	b	d	c	a	◇c	a	d	○d	△b	□c	34
CTR E-56	b	c	d	a	◇a	○c	b	d	△d	□b	40
CTR E-57	d	a	○b	○c	○c	○b	a	d	△b	□d	46
CTR E-58	c	d	○a	b	d	a	c	○c	△a	□c	52
CTR E-59	c	c	a	◇d	○b	○a	d	b	△c	□a	58
CTR E-60	d	○a	c	d	○b	○c	a	d	△c	□a	64

○ = Inference (not said straight out, but you know from what is said)

◇ = sequence

△ = Another name for the story

□ = Main idea of the story

NOTES

VOCABULARY CHECK ANSWER KEY

Lessons CTR 506-51 to CTR 506-60

LESSON NUMBER		PAGE NUMBER

51 SAXON MEETS NORMAN 11

I.
1. blond
2. merchant
3. tournament
4. bog
5. armor
6. cloak

II.
1. c
2. d
3. a
4. b
5. c
6. a

52 VICTORY TO AN UNKNOWN KNIGHT 17

I.
1. defeat
2. yelp
3. thrust
4. mighty
5. helmet
6. shield

II.
1. c
2. c
3. a
4. b
5. c
6. b

53 DEBTS ARE PAID 23

I.
1. advise
2. squire
3. otherwise
4. purse
5. repay
6. nimble

II.
```
M  N  I  M  S  Q  O  J  A  R
A  D  V  I  N  E  T  B  L  E
E  R  E  P  A  L  H  N  I  M
O  T  H  E  R  R  E  P  A  Y
N  I  M  B  P  U  R  S  E  X
B  N  I  M  L  L  W  S  Q  R
S  A  R  P  U  R  I  R  U  P
Q  D  E  G  N  O  S  O  T  H
U  S  Q  U  I  R  E  P  A  Y
A  D  V  I  M  W  O  A  D  V
N  I  M  L  B  C  T  Y  I  S
B  L  I  M  L  U  H  D  V  P
X  C  U  R  E  P  E  R  S  A
L  A  U  M  O  T  N  W  E  W
```

VOCABULARY CHECK ANSWER KEY

Lessons CTR 506-51 to CTR 506-60

54 A CHAMPION IS WOUNDED

I.
1. severe
2. sunk
3. thrown
4. slash
5. vicious
6. mercy

II.
1. thrown, c
2. mercy, d
3. slash, f
4. vicious, a
5. sunk, b
6. severe, e

55 BAD NEWS FOR PRINCE JOHN

I.
1. delay
2. splendid
3. separate
4. release
5. attend
6. heal

II.

```
                    ¹·S       ²·S
                      E         P
                      P         L
  ¹·R E L E A S E      E
                      R         N
          ³·H        ²·D E L A Y
            E         T       I
          ³·A T T E N D       D
            L
```

56 A CASTLE FALLS

I.
1. traitor
2. broad
3. balcony
4. consent
5. twilight
6. clerk

II.
1. a
2. b
3. c
4. b
5. b
6. c

VOCABULARY CHECK ANSWER KEY

Lessons CTR 506-51 to CTR 506-60

LESSON NUMBER		PAGE NUMBER

57 A WITCH TRIAL FOR REBECCA   47

I.
1. cell
2. trial
3. presence
4. sob
5. plead
6. consider

II.
1. c
2. d
3. a
4. f
5. b
6. e

58 TO BURN AT THE STAKE   53

I.
1. volunteer
2. failure
3. justice
4. oppose
5. concern
6. glory

II.
1. duty
2. support
3. pity
4. final
5. obey
6. coax

59 FAREWELL TO ATHELSTANE   59

I.
1. accompany
2. seek
3. occasion
4. elm
5. solid
6. pierce

II.
1. NO
2. YES
3. YES
4. NO
5. YES
6. YES

VOCABULARY CHECK ANSWER KEY

Lessons CTR 506-51 to CTR 506-60

I.
1. cape
2. pardon
3. torch
4. drain
5. lurch
6. monk

II.
1. b
2. b
3. a
4. a
5. a
6. b